Dark as a Midnight Dream

POETRY COLLECTION 2

Compiled by
FIONA WATERS

Illustrated by
ZARA SLATTERY

Evans **EVANS BROTHERS LIMITED**

CONTENTS

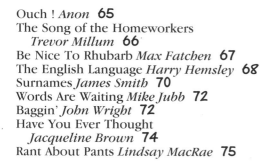

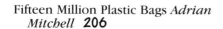

I SO LIKED SPRING

I so liked Spring last year
     Because you were here; -
       The thrushes too -
Because it was these you so liked to hear -
      I so liked you.

  This year's a different thing, -
     I'll not think of you.
But I'll like Spring because it is simply Spring
     As the thrushes do.

Charlotte Mew

HOME THOUGHTS FROM ABROAD

Oh, to be in England
Now that April's there,
And whoever wakes in England
Sees, some morning, unaware,
That the lowest boughs and the brushwood sheaf
Round the elm-tree bole are in tiny leaf,
While the chaffinch sings on the orchard bough
In England - now!

And after April, when May follows,
And the whitethroat builds, and all the swallows!
Hark, where my blossomed pear-tree in the hedge
Leans to the field and scatters on the clover
Blossoms and dewdrops - at the bent spray's edge -
That's the wise thrush; he sings each song twice over,
Lest you should think he never could recapture
The first fine careless rapture!

And though the fields look rough with hoary dew
All will be gay when noontide wakes anew
The buttercups, the little children's dower
Far brighter than this gaudy melon-flower!

Robert Browning

ADLESTROP

Yes. I remember Adlestrop -
The name, because one afternoon
Of heat the express-train drew up there
Unwontedly. It was late June.

The steam hissed. Someone cleared his throat.
No one left and no one came
On the bare platform. What I saw
Was Adlestrop - only the name

And willows, willow-herb, and grass,
And meadowsweet, and haycocks dry,
No whit less still and lonely fair
Than the high cloudlets in the sky.

And for that minute a blackbird sang
Close by, and round him, mistier,
Farther and farther, all the birds
Of Oxfordshire and Gloucestershire.

Edward Thomas

MUSHROOMS

Overnight, very
Whitely, discreetly,
Very quietly
Our toes, our noses
Take hold on the loam,
Acquire the air.

Nobody sees us,
Stops us, betrays us;
The small grains make room.

Soft fists insist on
Heaving the needles,
The leafy bedding,

Even the paving.
Our hammers, our rams,
Earless and eyeless,

Perfectly voiceless,
Widen the crannies,
Shoulder through holes. We

Diet on water,
On crumbs of shadow,
Bland-mannered, asking

Little or nothing.
So many of us!
So many of us!

We are shelves, we are
Tables, we are meek,
We are edible,

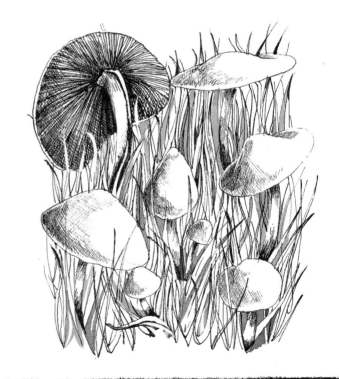

Nudgers and shovers
In spite of ourselves,
Our kind multiplies;

We shall by morning
Inherit the earth.
Our foot's in the door.

Sylvia Plath

READING A BONFIRE, TOP TO BOTTOM

Sparks expire just as they meet the stars.
Smoke thins out, dissolved in air.
Fingers of smoke in sparking gloves reach up.
Smoke as thick as wrists wrestles into darkness.
Tips of flame singe late-wandering insects.
Great fists of flame punch bales of smoke into the sky.
Guy's hat tilted and burns like hair.
The face is a bubbling horror-mask.
Buttons are popping off like fireworks.
He wears a coat of flame and ruin.
The rest of him has sunk into the furnace.
Here the heart's so hot, to look would burn your eyes.
Chestnuts and baked potatoes sweat and crack.
Already ash is piling up like white-hot snow.
The grass that grew here will be slow to come again,
Tomorrow all we'll know is a patch of scorched earth.

Geoffrey Summerfield

THE WAY THROUGH THE WOODS

They shut the road through the woods
Seventy years ago.
Weather and rain have undone it again,
And now you would never know
There was once a road through the woods
Before they planted the trees.
It is underneath the coppice and heath,
And the thin anemones.
Only the keeper sees
That, where the ring-dove broods,
And the badgers roll at ease,
There was once a road through the woods.

Yet, if you enter the woods
Of a summer evening late,
When the night-air cools on the trout-ringed pools
Where the otter whistles his mate
(They fear not men in the woods,
Because they see so few),
You will hear the beat of a horse's feet,
And the swish of a skirt in the dew,
Steadily cantering through
The misty solitudes,
As though they perfectly knew
The old lost road through the woods ...
But there is no road through the woods!

Rudyard Kipling

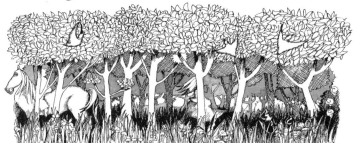

SONG OF THE OPEN ROAD

I wish to sing the joys of hiking;
It is superior to biking.
I know it is not quite so fast -
That only makes the pleasure last.
Heigh-ho! When springtime is in bud
How jolly then to plough through mud,
To clump along like happy vagrants
And sniff the petrol fumes' sweet fragrance,
As motor cars go flashing past
With honk of horn and klaxon blast.
In winter-time there's nothing like
A good old-fashioned ten-mile hike;
We love to march through rain and sleet
With leaky boots upon our feet,
Our clothes each moment growing wetter,
And if there's hail, that's even better.
And then when summer comes, how gay
Our trek along the broad highway,
With songs upon our dusty lips
And cheery words and merry quips.
When gazing down sweet pastoral vistas
We cannot even think of blisters.
In any weather dry or damp,
There's nothing like a day-long tramp
To make us feel that life is sweet
In spite of corns and aching …
Hey, mister, give us a lift!

R. D. Fairburn

AUTUMN SONG

There came a day that caught the summer
Wrung its neck
Plucked it
And ate it.

Now what shall I do with the trees?
The day said, the day said.
Strip them bare, strip them bare.
Let's see what is really there.

And what shall I do with the sun?
The day said, the day said.
Roll him away till he's cold and small.
He'll come back rested if he comes back at all.

And what shall I do with the birds?
The day said, the day said.
The birds I've frightened, let them flit,
I'll hang out pork for the brave tomtit.

And what shall I do with the seed?
The day said, the day said.
Bury it deep, see what it's worth.
See if it can stand the earth.

What shall I do with the people?
The day said, the day said.
Stuff them with apple and blackberry pie -
They'll love me then till the day they die.

There came this day and he was autumn.
His mouth was wide
And red as a sunset.
His tail was an icicle.

Ted Hughes

WINTER

Sweet blackbird is silenced with chaffinch and thrush,
Only waistcoated robin still chirps in the bush:
Soft sun-loving swallows have mustered in force,
And winged to the spice-teeming southlands their course.

Plump housekeeper dormouse has tucked himself neat,
Just a brown ball in moss with a morsel to eat:
Armed hedgehog has huddled him into the hedge,
While frogs scarce miss freezing deep down in the sedge.

Soft swallows have left us alone in the lurch,
But robin sits whistling to us from his perch:
If I were red robin I'd pipe you a tune,
Would make you despise all the beauties of June.

But, since that cannot be, let us draw round the fire,
Munch chestnuts, tell stories, and stir the blaze higher:
We'll comfort pinched robin with crumbs, little man,
Till he'll sing us the very best song that he can.

Christina Rossetti

IT IS SNOWING

It is snowing
it is snowing
and the world is white
white
white
snow falls from the sky
in small drops
in big drops
in whole showersful
sometimes it is gentle
and plays with you
it falls softly on your nose
sometimes it falls so hard
you want to cry
Sometimes it becomes a blizzard
a storm
and you cannot go to school
or out to play
you watch the storm from your window
with your nose pressed against it
When the snow settles
you can ski
skate
go tobogganing
or make a snowman or woman

In Spanish snow is la nieve
In Swahili snow is Theluji
and
In French snow is la neige
The Inuit people have 22 different names for snow

Afua Cooper

EXPLORER

Two o'clock:
Let out of the back door of the house, our cat
Is practising the snow.

The layer of white makes a small, straight, crumbling cliff
Where we open the back door inwards. The cat
Sniffs it with suspicion, learns you can just about
Pat the flaking snow with a careful dab. Then,
A little bolder, he dints it with one whole foot
- and withdraws it, curls it as if slightly lame,

And looks down at it, oddly. The snow is
Different from anything else, not like
A rug, or a stretch of lino, or an armchair to claw upon
And be told to *Get off!*

The snow is peculiar, but not forbidden. The cat
Is welcome to go out in the snow. Does
The snow welcome the cat?
He thinks, looks, tries again.

Three paces out of the door, his white feet find
You sink a little way all the time, it is slow and cold, but it
Doesn't particularly hurt. Perhaps you can even enjoy it,
as something new.
So he walks on, precisely, on the tips of very cautious paws ...

Half-past three, the cat stretched warm indoors.
From the bedroom window we can see his explorations
- From door to fence, from fence to gate, from gate to wall
to tree, and back,
Are long pattered tracks and trade
-routes of round paw-marks
Which fresh snow is
quietly filling.

Alan Brownjohn

FOR SALE

Four hundred years this little house has stood
Through wind and fire, through earthquake and through
    flood;
Still its old beams, though bulged and warped, are strong,
In spite of gaping wounds both deep and long.
The doors are low and give such narrow space
We must walk humbly in this little place.
The windows here, no longer square or straight,
Are able now, from their fantastic state,
To squint down their own walls, and see the flowers
That get more drippings from the eaves than showers.
Six hundred pounds for all this precious stone!
These little, quaint old windows squinting down;
This orchard, with its apples' last appeal
To dumpling or sweet cider; this deep well,
Whose little eye has sparkled from its birth -
Four hundred years in sixty feet of earth!

W.H. Davies

A STRIKING OLD MAN

When grandfather first came to us
We did not know how old he was
Nor how reliable.
Regular as clockwork he wound up our day
And simply by his presence
Reminded us of things we had not done.
Not that he ever complained
And we liked him for that.

They had got tired of him at the other house,
So he arrived unceremoniously one afternoon in a van,
They said he had been too much trouble,
He hardly fitted their way of life.
We came to love him.
On his face you could see what time had done
And quite a lot that had defeated time.
Sometimes his secrets were unlocked.
Then we could see right through
To the frailty and simplicity
Of something that had gone on working
Through so many changes.
His voice was occasionally sharp
But we knew he was just run down
And so we would make allowances.
Adjustments were easy.
For much of the day he was quiet
And we heard him mostly at night
Breathing throughout the house
In a satisfied old-fashioned way.
When visitors came he was good:
We saw them admiring his hands -
He had a certain veneer.
In time he was part of our lives.
The children lived by his looks.
He made us all feel at home.

Alasdair Ashton

POSTING LETTERS

There are no lamps in our village,
And when the owl-and-bat black night
Creeps up low fields
And sidles along the manor walls
I walk quickly.

It is winter;
The letters patter from my hand
Into the tin box in the cottage wall;
The gate taps behind me,
And the road in the sliver of moonlight
Gleams greasily
Where the tractors have stood.

I have to go under the spread fingers of the trees
Under the dark windows of the old man's house,
Where the panes in peeling frames
Flash like spectacles
As I tip-toe.
But there is no sound of him in his one room
In the Queen-Anne shell,
Behind the shutters.

I run past the gates,
Their iron feet gaitered with grass,
Into the church porch,
Perhaps for sanctuary,
Standing, hand on the cold door ring,
While above
The tongue-tip of the clock
Clops
Against the hard palate of the tower.

The door groans as I push
And
Dare myself to dash
Along the flagstones to the great brass bird,
To put one shrinking hand
Upon the gritty lid
Of Black Tom's tomb.

Don't tempt whatever spirits stir
In this damp corner,
But
Race down the aisle,
Blunder past font,
Fumble the door,
Leap steps,
Clang iron gate,
And patter through the short-cut muddy lane.

Oh, what a pumping of breath
And choking throat
For three letters.
And now there are the cattle
Stirring in the straw
So close
I can hear their soft muzzling and coughs;
And there are the bungalows,
And the steel-blue miming of the little screen;
And the familiar rattle of the latch,
And our own knocker
Clicking like an old friend;
And
I am home.

Gregory Harrison

THE EMPTY HOUSE

Where the lone wind on the hilltop
Shakes the thistles as it passes,
Stirs the quiet-ticking grasses
That keep time outside the door,
Stands a house that's grey and silent;
No one lives there any more.

Wending through the broken windows,
Every season and its weather
Whisper in those rooms together:
Summer's warm and wandering rains
Rot the leaves of last year's autumn,
Warp the floors that winter stains.

In a papered hall a clock-shape,
Dim and pale on yellowed flowers,
Still remains where rang the hours
Of a clock that's lost and gone.
And the fading ghost keeps no-time
On the wall it lived upon.

On a stairway where no footsteps
Stir the dusty sunlight burning
Sit the patient shadows turning
Speechless faces to the wall
While they hear the silent striking
Of that no-clock in the hall.

Russell Hoban

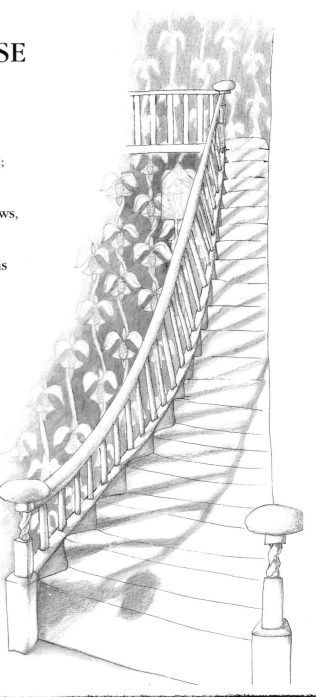

DOOR HAS TWO FACES

Door
has two faces

one looks without
at wind and rain

it has a bell
a brass knocker

and a slit
for eyes and words to pass

the other looks within
at a fireside

it has a latch
an iron bolt

and maybe a hook
for hanging up a coat

if there were no door
there would be no face

the carpet would be
ankle-deep in snow

and muffins would be
toasted on the street

so let us praise what
keeps two worlds apart

until we choose to pass
from one to the other

Keith Bosley

THE TREES ARE DOWN

They are cutting down the great plane-trees at the end of the gardens.
For days there has been the grate of the saw, the swish of the branches as
    they fall,
The crash of the trunks, the rustle of trodden leaves,
With the 'Whoops' and the 'Whoas,' the loud common talk, the loud
    common laughs of the men, above it all.

I remember one evening of a long past Spring
Turning in at a gate, getting out of a cart, and finding a large dead rat in
    the mud of the drive.
I remember thinking: alive or dead, a rat was a god-forsaken thing,
But at least, in May, that even a rat should be alive.

The week's work here is as good as done. There is just one bough
  On the roped bole, in the fine grey rain,
      Green and high
      And lonely against the sky.
        (Down now! -)
      And but for that,
      If an old dead rat
Did once, for a moment, unmake the Spring, I might never have thought of
    him again.

It is not for a moment the Spring is unmade today;
These were great trees, it was in them from root to stem:
When the men with the 'Whoops' and the 'Whoas' have carted the whole
    of the whispering loveliness away
Half the Spring, for me, will have gone with them.

It is going now, and my heart has been struck with the hearts of the planes;
Half my life it has beat with these, in the sun, in the rains,
    In the March wind, the May breeze,

In the great gales that came over to them across the roofs from the great seas.
    There was only a quiet rain when they were dying;
    They must have heard the sparrows flying,
And the small creeping creatures in the earth where they were lying -
    But I, all day, I heard an angel crying:
        'Hurt not the trees.'

Charlotte Mew

THE DARKENING GARDEN

Where have all the colours gone?

Red of roses, green of grass,
Brown of tree-trunk, gold of cowslip,
Pink of poppy, blue of cornflower,
Who among you saw them pass?

They have gone to make the sunset:

Broidered on the western sky,
All the colours of our garden,
Woven into a lovely curtain,
Over the bed where Day doth die.

Anonymous

BIG FEARS

Twenty-five feet above Sîan's house
hangs a thick wire cable
that droops and sags between two
electricity pylons.
A notice says it carries 40,000 volts
from one metallic scarecrow to the next,
then on to the next and the next
right across the countryside to the city.
The cable sways above Sian's council house
making her radio crackle and sometimes
making her television go on the blink.

If it's a very windy night
Sian gets frightened because she
thinks the cable might snap,
fall onto the roof and electrocute
everyone as they sleep.

This is Sîan's Big Fear.

Outside Matthew's bedroom there
is a tall tree. Taller than the house.
In summer it is heavy with huge leaves.
In winter it stands lonely as a morning moon.

On a windy night, Matthew worries
that the tree might be blown down
and crash through his bedroom window.
It would certainly kill him and his cat
if it wasn't in its own cardboard box.

This is Matthew's Big Fear.

Outside Karen's bedroom there's nothing
but a pleasant view, meadows, hedges, sheep
and some distance gentle hills.
There's nothing sinister, nothing to worry about.

But in the dark Karen thinks
the darting shapes on the ceiling
are really the shadows of a ghost's
great cold hands and that the night noises
made by the water pipes are the
screeches and groans of attic skeletons.

John Rice

MORNING AFTER A STORM

There was a roaring in the wind all night;
The rain came heavily and fell in floods;
But now the sun is rising calm and bright;
The birds are singing in the distant woods;
Over his own sweet voice the stock-dove broods;
The jay makes answer as the Magpie chatters;
And all the air is filled with pleasant noise of waters.

All things that love the sun are out of doors;
The sky rejoices in the morning's birth;
The grass is bright with rain-drops - on the moors
The hare is running races in her mirth;
And with her feet she from the plashy earth
Raises a mist, that, glittering in the sun,
Runs with her all the way, wherever she doth run.

William Wordsworth

PETALS

Last night's wind has blown off all the peach blossoms in the garden.
Child, you want to sweep the flowers away:
Aren't the fallen petals flowers?
    Why not leave them alone?

Anonymous

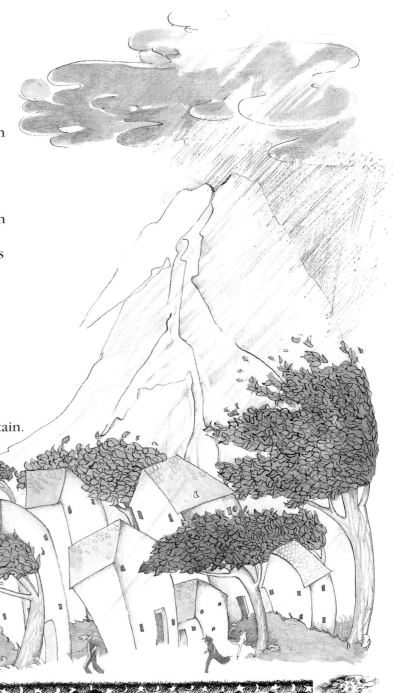

HURRICANE

Shut the windows
Bolt the doors
Big rain coming
Climbing up the mountain

Neighbours whisper
Dark clouds gather
Big rain coming
Climbing up the mountain

Gather in the clothes lines
Pull down the blinds
Big wind rising
Coming up the mountain

Branches falling
Raindrops flying
Tree tops swaying
People running
Big wind blowing
Hurricane! on the mountain.

Dionne Brand

THERE ARE NO PEOPLE SONG

You say there were no people.
    Smoke was spreading over the earth.
You say there were no people.
    Smoke was spreading.

First Man was the very first to emerge, they say,
    Smoke was spreading.
He brought with him the various robes and precious things,
  they say,
    Smoke was spreading.
He brought with him the white corn and the yellow corn,
  they say,
    Smoke was spreading.
He brought with him the various animals and the growing things,
  they say,
    Smoke was spreading.

You say there were no people.
    Smoke was spreading.
First Woman was the very first to emerge, they say,
    Smoke was spreading.
She brought with her the various precious things and robes,
  they say,
    Smoke was spreading.
She brought with her the yellow corn and the varicolored corn,
  they say,
    Smoke was spreading.
She brought with her the various animals and the growing things,
  they say,
    Smoke was spreading.

You say there were no people.
    Smoke was spreading.
You say there were no people.
    Smoke was spreading.

Navaho Tribe

LANDSCAPE AS WEREWOLF

Near here, the last grey wolf
In England was clubbed down. Still,
After two hundred years, the same pinched wind
Rakes through his cairn of bones

As he squats quiet, watching daylight seep
Away from the scarred granite, and its going drain
The hills' bare faces. Far below,
A tiny bus twists on its stringy path
And scuttles home around a darkening bend.

The fells contract, regroup in starker forms;
Dusk tightens on them, as the wind gets up
And stretches hungrily: tensed at the nape,
The course heath bristles like a living pelt.

The sheep are all penned in. Down at the pub
They sing, and shuttle darts: the hostellers
Dubbin their heavy boots. Above the crags
The first stars prick their eyes and bide their time.

William Dunlop

THE FLINT

Who lived in these ancient woods?
Many thousand years ago
small men made their dwellings here -
lugged the great stones to and fro
and beneath a sheltering bough
ate, and slept, as I do now.

Who last held this flint? I guess
someone sharpened it to be
a precious weapon … kept it safe …
used it often, skilfully,
carved an arrowhead, and slit
the creature's throat he slew with it.

Who felt spirits in the trees?
Saw the sun rise like a god
on its journey east to west?
Who sniffed water, understood
where it wandered through the ground
and marked the spot it might be found?

Who walked on this ancient track?
Short and muscular, he wore
skins to cover him, and lit
fires to warm the winter's core.
In my hand (how strange it is!)
I hold the flint he held in his.

Jean Kenward

WINDY GAP

As I was going through Windy Gap
A hawk and a cloud hung over the map.

The land lay bare and the wind blew loud
And the hawk cried out from the heart of the cloud,

'Before I fold my wings in sleep
I'll pick the bones of your travelling sheep,

For the leaves blow black and the wintry sun
Shows the trees' white skeleton.'

A magpie sat in the tree's high top
Singing a song on Windy Gap

That streamed far down to the plain below
Like a shaft of light from a high window.

From the bending tree he sang aloud,
And the sun shone out of the heart of the cloud.

And it seemed to me as we travelled through
That my sheep were the notes that trumpet blew.

And so I sing this song of praise
For travelling sheep and blowing days.

David Campbell

THROUGH THAT DOOR

Through that door
Is a garden with a wall,
The red brick crumbling,
The lupins growing tall,
Where the lawn is like a carpet
Spread for you,
And it's all as tranquil
As you never knew.

Through that door
Is the great ocean-sea
Which heaves and rolls
To eternity,
With its islands and promontories
Waiting for you
To explore and discover
In that vastness of blue.

Through that door
Is your secret room
Where the window lets in
The light of the moon,
With its mysteries and magic
Where you can find
Thrills and excitements
of every kind.

Through that door
Are the mountains and the moors
And the rivers and the forests
Of the great outdoors,
All the plains and the ice-caps
And the lakes as blue as sky
For all those creatures
That walk or swim or fly.

Through that door
Is the city of the mind
Where you can imagine
What you'll find.
You can make of that city
What you want it to,
And if you choose to share it,
Then it could come true.

John Cotton

THE ALCHEMIST

There's a mysterious light
Burns all through the night
In that house where some people say
The alchemist dwells
With books full of spells
And a cat who scares children away.

Some say that he lives
In that house all alone
Some say he has claws and a beak
Some say he keeps rats
And vampire bats
And a raven he's taught how to speak.

And the children play dare:
'I dare you to spy
Through the dust on his window pane.'
They say those who dare
To enter his lair
Have never been seen again.

They say that his furnace
Turns iron and bronze
Into ingots of glistening gold..
They say if you take
The powder he makes
You'll never fall sick or grow old.

Some say he's a wizard
Some say he's a saint
Some say he eats toads for his tea
So I don't think I'll pay
Him a visit today
For fear he should want to eat me.

Gareth Owen

GREEN MAN IN THE GARDEN

Green man in the garden
    Staring from the tree,
Why do you look so long and hard
Through the pane at me?

Your eyes are dark as holly,
    Of sycamore your horns,
Your bones are made of elder-branch,
    Your teeth are made of thorns.

Your hat is made of ivy-leaf,
    Of bark your dancing shoes,
And evergreen and green and green
    Your jacket and shirt and trews.

Leave your house and leave your land
    And throw away the key,
And never look behind, he creaked,
    And come and live with me.

I bolted up the window,
    I bolted up the door,
I drew the blind that I should find
    The green man never more.

But when I softly turned the stair
    As I went up to bed,
I saw the green man standing there.
    Sleep well, my friend, he said.

Charles Causley

OLD MEN OF MAGIC

Old men of magic
with beards long and aged,
speak tales on evenings,
tales so entrancing,
we sit and we listen,
to whispery secrets
about the earth and the heavens.
And late at night,
after sundown they speak
of spirits that live
in silk cotton trees,
of frightening shadows
that sneak through the dark,
and bright balls of fire
that fly in night air,
of shapes unimaginable,
we gasp and we gape,
then just as we're scared
old men of magic
wave hands rough and wrinkled
and all trace of fear disappears.

Dionne Brand

I know a bank where the wild thyme blows,
Where oxlips and the nodding violet grows,
Quite overcanopied with luscious woodbine,
With sweet musk-roses, and with eglantine.
There sleeps Titania sometime of the night,
Lulled in these flowers with dances and delight;
And there the snake throws her enamelled skin,
Weed wide enough to wrap a fairy in.

William Shakespeare   *from A Midsummer Night's Dream*

OVERHEARD ON A SALTMARSH

Nymph, nymph, what are your beads?

Green glass, goblin. Why do you stare at them?

Give them me.

No.

Give them me. Give them me.

      No.

Then I will howl all night in the reeds,
Lie in the mud and howl for them.

Goblin, why do you love them so?
They are better than stars or water,
Better than voices of winds that sing,
Better than any man's fair daughter,
Your green glass beads on a silver ring.

Hush, I stole them out of the moon.

Give me your beads, I want them.
      No.

I will howl in a deep lagoon
For your green glass beads, I love them so.
Give them me. Give them.

      No.

Harold Monro

WITCHES GATHER

Dame, dame! the watch is set:
Quickly come, we all are met.
From the lakes and from the fens,
From the rocks and from the dens,
From the woods and from the caves,
From the churchyards, from the graves,
From the dungeon, from the tree
That they die on, here are we!

The weather is fair, the wind is good:
Up, dame, on your horse of wood!
Or else tuck up your grey frock,
And saddle your goat or your green cock,
And make his bridle a ball of thread
To toll up how many miles you have rid.
Quickly come away,
For we all stay.

The owl is abroad, the bat and the toad,
        And so is the cat-a-mountain;
The ant and the mole sit both in a hole,
        And the frog peeps out of the fountain.
The dogs they do bay, and the timbrels play,
        The spindle is now a-turning;
The moon it is red, and the stars are fled,
        But the sky is a-burning.

Ben Jonson

MRS McQUEEN

She keeps a pet peacock
to chase off black cats;
she walks under ladders,
steps on all cracks.

She opens her brolly
inside the front door;
she won't cross her fingers,
says it's a bore!

Her mirror is crazed
as an egg in a cup;
on her door hangs a horseshoe -
bottom-side up.

Her vases are filled
with sweet-smelling may
and six peacock feathers
stare from her bay.

She throws away wishbones,
won't have mistletoe;
buys lucky mince pies -
to feed her pet crow.

Born on a Friday,
one dark Hallowe'en;
she moved on St Swithin's
dressed all in green.

She's all right so far
from what I have seen -
but I would touch wood
if I lived at Thirteen!

Judith Nicholls

Now the hungry lion roars,
      And the wolf behowls the moon;
Whilst the heavy ploughman snores,
      All with weary task fordone.
Now the wasted brands do glow,
      Whilst the screech-owl, screeching loud,
Puts the wretch that lies in woe
      In remembrance of a shroud.
Now it is the time of night
      That the graves, all gaping wide,
Every one lets forth his sprite,
      In the church-way paths to glide:
And we fairies, that do run
      By the triple Hecate's team,
From the presence of the sun,
      Following darkness like a dream,
Now are frolic: not a mouse
Shall disturb this hallow'd house:
I am sent with broom before,
To sweep the dust behind the door.

William Shakespeare   *from A Midsummer Night's Dream*

FEAR OF THE DARK

Along the unlit lane on a night
When the stars are blind, the moon masked,
Footsteps follow. I knew a man
Of six foot three who, on dark nights,
Held two lit cigarettes between his lips
Hoping by this bright stratagem
To fox footpads, mislead murderers.
I used to laugh at him, but not now.
I clench teeth and fists and walk fast.
When I reach the house I switch on lights.

The darkness seems defeated, yet
Open the door, the light does not flow far
Beyond the threshold; it stops dead
A few feet from the step, I hear
The darkness growing; it is enormous.
It is in this room in thin disguise.
I am afraid of it, and with good reason.

Vernon Scannell

RUMOUR

Somebody is whispering on the stair.
What are those words half spoken, half drawn back?
Whence are those muffled words, some red, some black?
Who is whispering? Who is there?

Somebody is sneaking up the stair,
His feet approaching every doorway,
Yet never a moment standing anywhere.

Now many whisper close outside some door.
O suddenly push it open wide.
You see: whoever said he heard them, he has lied.

And yet words are left dark like heavy dust
In many rooms, or red on iron like rust:
And who contrives to leave them? Someone must.

In every street, this noisy town of ours
Has stealthy whispering watchers walking round,
Recording all our movements, every sound,
Hissing and shuffling, and they may have found
Today my name: tomorrow they'll find yours.

Harold Monro

HIDE AND SEEK

Call out. Call loud: 'I'm ready! Come and find me!'
The sacks in the toolshed smell like the seaside.
They'll never find you in this salty dark,
But be careful that your feet aren't sticking out.
Wiser not to risk another shout.
The floor is cold. They'll probably be searching
The bushes near the swing. Whatever happens
You mustn't sneeze when they come prowling in.
And here they are, whispering at the door;
You've never heard them sound so hushed before.
Don't breathe. Don't move. Stay dumb. Hide in your
blindness.
They're moving closer, someone stumbles, mutters;
Their words and laughter scuffle, and they're gone.
But don't come out just yet; they'll try the lane
And then the greenhouse and back here again.
They must be thinking that you're very clever.
Getting more puzzled as they search all over.
It seems a long time since they went away.
Your legs are stiff, the cold bites through your coat;
The dark damp smell of sand moves in your throat.
It's time to let them know that you're the winner.
Push off the sacks. Uncurl and stretch. That's better!
Out of the shed and call to them: 'I've won!
Here I am! Come and own up I've caught you!'
The darkening garden watches. Nothing stirs.
The bushes hold their breath; the sun is gone.
Yes, here you are. But where are they who sought you?

Vernon Scannell

THE FACE AT THE WINDOW

I used to catch the bus to school alone
On a corner where the wind blew from the shore
There was a church, and where I had to stand
A garage where they brought crashed cars to mend.
And one day, early morning as I stood
And watched the traffic on the quiet road
I saw a face in one of the crashed cars
Whose door and wing and seats were torn apart
I knew that there was no-one in the place
And yet in that crashed car I saw a face.
I didn't want to look and yet I must
And each glance brought the moment of that crash.
I knew exactly what the girl was like
Twenty or so, and pretty, and her look
Told me how suddenly the crash had come
Her mouth was barely opening to scream
She couldn't close her eyes or turn her head
Or stop that moment. And was she dead?
I couldn't turn away or look at her
The car was empty yet the face was there.
It stayed in front of me all day at school
Next day I said I mustn't look, but still
The woman's face was there in that crashed car
And she and I touched hands with that same fear
And every day that week we shared a glance
That stopped our breath and chilled our blood to ice.
Asleep or waking I would know that face.
That smashed against the windscreen with such force
That her make-up had been pressed into the glass
And into my memory, never to be erased.

Berlie Doherty

PRINCE KANO

In a dark wood Prince Kano lost his way
And searched in vain through the long summer's day.
At last, when night was near, he came in sight
Of a small clearing filled with yellow light,
And there, bending beside his brazier, stood
A charcoal burner wearing a black hood.
The Prince cried out for joy: 'Good friend, I'll give
What you will ask: guide me to where I live.'
The man pulled back his hood: he had no face -
Where it should be there was an empty space.

Half dead with fear the Prince staggered away,
Rushed blindly through the wood till break of day;
And then he saw a larger clearing, filled
With houses, people; but his soul was chilled,
He looked around for comfort, and his search
Led him inside a small, half-empty church
Where monks prayed. 'Father,' to one he said,
'I've seen a dreadful thing; I am afraid.'
'What did you see, my son?' 'I saw a man
Whose face was like ...' and, as the Prince began,
The monk drew back his hood and seemed to hiss,
Pointing to where his face should be, 'Like this?'

Edward Lowbury

UNWELCOME

We were young, we were merry, we were very very wise,
    And the door stood open at our feast,
When there passed us a woman with the West in her eyes,
    And a man with his back to the East.

O, still grew the hearts that were beating so fast,
    The loudest voice was still.
The jest died away on our lips as they passed,
    And the rays of July struck chill.

The cups of red wine turn'd pale on the board,
    The white bread black as soot.
The hound forgot the hand of her lord,
    She fell down at his foot.

Low let me lie, where the dead dog lies,
    Ere I sit me down again at a feast,
When there passes a woman with the West in her eyes,
    And a man with his back to the East.

Mary Coleridge

CAPTIVE'S SONG

Where can I go
That I might live forever?
Where can I go
That I might live forever?
The old fathers have gone to the spirit-land,
 Where can I go
 That we might live together?

Omaha Tribe

SOLITUDE

Laugh, and the world laughs with you,
 Weep, and you weep alone,
For sad old earth must borrow its mirth,
 But has trouble enough of its own.
Sing, and the hills will answer;
 Sigh, it is lost on the air,
The echoes bound to a joyful sound,
 But shrink from voicing care.

Rejoice, and men will seek you;
 Grieve, and they turn and go.
They want full measure of all your pleasure.
 But they do not need your woe.
Be glad, and your friends are many,
 Be sad, and you lose them all;
There are none to decline your nectared wine,
 But alone you must drink life's gall.

Feast, and your halls are crowded,
 Fast, and the world goes by.
Succeed and give - and it helps you live,

But no man can help you die;
There is room in the halls of pleasure
    For the large and lordly train,
But one by one we must all file on
    Through the narrow aisles of pain.

Ella Wheeler Wilcox

THE THANKSGIVINGS

We who are here present thank the Great Spirit that we are here to
    praise Him.
We thank Him that He has created men and women, and ordered that
    these beings shall always be living to multiply the earth.
We thank Him for making the earth and giving these beings its
    products to live on.
We thank Him for the water that comes out of the earth and runs
    for our lands.
We thank Him for all the animals on the earth.
We thank Him for certain timbers that grow and have fluids coming
    from them for us all.
We thank Him for the branches of the trees that grow shadows for
    our shelter.
We thank Him for the beings that come from the west, the thunder
    and lightning that water the earth.
We thank Him for the light which we call our oldest brother, the sun
    that works for our good.
We thank Him for all the fruits that grow on the trees and vines.
We thank Him for his goodness in making the forest, and thank all
    its trees.
Who is our friend?   The Thunder is our friend.
Who is our friend?   The Thunder is our friend.
Who is our friend?   The Bull is our friend.

Iroquois Tribe

GAELIC BLESSING

Deep peace of the running wave to you.
Deep peace of the flowing air to you.
Deep peace of the quiet air to you.
Deep peace of the shining stars to you.
Deep peace of the Son of Peace to you.

PRAYER FOR PEACE

Lord, make me a channel of Thy peace that, where there is hatred, I may bring
love; that where there is wrong, I may bring the spirit of forgiveness; that where
there is discord, I may bring harmony; that, where there is error, I may bring truth;
that, where there is doubt, I may bring faith; that, where there is despair, I may
bring hope; that, where there are shadows, I may bring light; that where there is
sadness, I may bring joy.

Lord, grant that I may seek rather to comfort than to be comforted, to understand
than to be understood; to love than to be loved; for it is by forgetting self that one
finds; it is by forgiving that one is forgiven; it is by dying that one awakens to
eternal life.

St Francis of Assisi

A DIFFERENT KIND OF SUNDAY

You go to church in England,
it isn't the bright Caribbean day,
isn't orange and mango ripening
with fowls raking about under bush.
It's not a donkey and mule holy day
after they'd bathed in sea in sunrise,

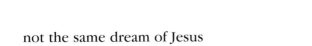

not the same dream of Jesus
when you are melting,
though you fan yourself and everybody else.

You go to church in England,
it's no banana and coconut trees
making a little breeze look merry
in midddleday sunhot
when goats pant in mottled shades.

You go to church in England,
cleaned-up people listen to parsons
but trucks aren't parked in palmtree yards
when loose boys fix bicycles,
birdsong stripes the day like ribbons,
the sea has a sabbath day seasound.

You go to church in England,
parson is same preacher-Paul strong-man
beating the air to beat up badness
but John-crows don't glide around blue sky
to be looked at out of window.
And good things at the end aren't
like best lemonade, iced up,
and dinner added-to all week
to go with family jokes kept Sunday-quiet
before the walking-out in evening shadows.

You go to church in England,
you sit in a groan
of traffic on and on around you,
where, O, the sun is so so forgetful.

_____
James Berry

THREE RUSTY NAILS

Mother, there's a strange man
Waiting at the door
With a familiar sort of face
You feel you've seen before.

Says his name is Jesus
Can we spare a couple of bob
Says he's been made redundant
And now can't find a job.

Yes I think he is a foreigner
Egyptian or a Jew
Oh aye, and that reminds me
He'd like some water too.

Well shall I give him what he wants
Or send him on his way?
OK I'll give him 5p
Say that's all we've got today.

And I'll forget about the water
I suppose it's a bit unfair
But honest, he's filthy dirty
All beard and straggly hair.

Mother, he asked about the water
I said the tank had burst
Anyway I gave him the money
That seemed to quench his thirst.

He said it was little things like that
That kept him on the rails
Then he gave me his autographed picture
And these three rusty nails.

Roger McGough

THE BISHOP'S MISTAKE

The bishop glanced through his window pane
On a world of sleet, and wind, and rain.
When a dreary figure met his eyes
That made the bishop soliloquize.

And as the bishop gloomily thought
He ordered pen and ink to be brought.
Then 'Providence Watches' he plainly wrote
And pinned the remark to a one-pound note.

Seizing his hat from his lordly rack
And wrapping his cloak around his back,
Across the road the bishop ran
And gave the note to the shabby man.

That afternoon was the bishop's 'At Home',
When everyone gathered beneath his dome,
Curate and canon from far and near
Came to partake of the bishop's cheer.

There in the good old bishop's hall
Stood a stranger lean and tall.
'Your winnings, my lord,' he cried. 'Well done -
'Providence Watches', at ten to one.'

It is to be noted on Sunday next
The bishop skilfully chose his text.
And from the pulpit earnestly told
Of the fertile seed that returned tenfold.

Anonymous

IS THE MOON TIRED?

Is the moon tired? She looks so pale
    Within her misty veil;
She scales the sky from east to west,
    And takes no rest.

Before the coming of the night
The moon shows papery white;
Before the dawning of the day
    She fades away.

Christina Rossetti

APPLEMOON

Something woke me: startle-sound
or moonlight. The house dreamt
like an old cat, but I
looked out my window.

And night was day in a midnight
moon-flood. Mazy moon
flaring a halo of quick clouds
running the big black sky.
And I saw a thousand windfall apples
lying luminous as sea-stones beached
below the spiky silver trees.

So, shivering I
mouse-went out
with a basket, barefoot, toes
curling in the cold;
and singing soft
took ripe reluctant apples
under close and curious stars.

Only soon I saw
my shadow was not
the same as I;
it stooped more -
had its own thinness ...
and our fingers
never met.

I quick-ran back
the house so
sleepy-warm, sure.
But looking out through curtain lace
I saw my shadow linger
moving slow and crooked, plucking
shadow apples
from the shining moony grass.

Rose Flint

BLAKE LEADS A WALK
ON THE MILKY WAY

He gave silver shoes to the rabbit
and golden gloves to the cat
and emerald boots to the tiger and me
and boots of iron to the rat.

He inquired, 'Is everyone ready?
The night is uncommonly cold.
We'll start on our journey as children,
but I fear we will finish it old.'

He hurried us to the horizon
where morning and evening meet.
The slippery stars went skipping
under our hapless feet.

'I'm terribly cold,' said the rabbit.
'My paws are becoming quite blue,
and what will become of my right thumb
while you admire the view?'

'The stars,' said the cat, 'are abundant
and falling on every side.
Let them carry us back to our comforts.
Let us take the stars for a ride.'

'I shall garland my room,' said the tiger,
'with a few of these emerald tights.'
'I shall give up sleeping forever,' I said.
'I shall never part day from night.'

The rat was sullen. He grumbled
he ought to have stayed in his bed.
'What's gathered by fools in heaven
will never endure,' he said.

Blake gave silver stars to the rabbit
and golden stars to the cat
and emerald stars to the tiger and me
but a handful of dirt to the rat.

_____

Nancy Willard

THE SONG OF THE STARS

We are the stars which sing,
We sing with our light;
We are the birds of fire,
We fly over the sky.
Our light is a voice;
We make a road for spirits,
For the spirits to pass over.
Among us are three hunters
Who chase a bear;
There never was a time
When they were not hunting.
We look down on the mountains.
This is the Song of the Stars.

_____

Passamaquoddy Tribe

THE TWILIGHT

You left before the twilight,
And I just wanted to tell you,
That the twilight was beautiful:
The sky a myriad of mysterious dark shades;
Tufts of snowy white and deep blue,
Racing to blot out the first stars,
Across the purple breathless sky.
And the shivering moon with its pale halo,
Reflected on the sea.

You should have stayed for the twilight,
If not for me.

Fabiola Smolowik (Aged 15)

DIFFERENT DREAMS

When dusk is done
And the grey has gone
And the stars blow out
That once were on,
Then the pale moon casts
Its frozen gleams
And the hollow of night
Fills up with dreams:
Cats of mice
Elves of trolls
Cooks of silver spoons and bowls.
Poets dream of winds to Rome.
Sailors dream of ships and home.
Princes dream of foreign lands
To conquer
And of ladies' hands.
Dogs dream dreams
Of hounds and hares
The red fox dreams
Of grass green lairs.
While deep in your sleep
With your dark eyes shut tight,
You dream of the day
That will follow the night.

Karla Kuskin

FEVER DREAM

Tossed with fever on my bed,
I thought the clock might wake the dead;
At twelve it struck so mad a din,
I wondered, would it strike thirteen?
Before that came I counted sheep
And had a dream in troubled sleep:
I looked across the road at night
And saw a window filled with light;
And someone looking out of it,
Whose face was in the shade, unlit,
Seemed to be looking back at me:
It was a face I had to see.
I tried and tried to pierce the shade,
And suddenly became afraid:
A light came on, and I could name
That person in the window frame:
His features scared me to the bone:
I looked again - they were my own!

Edward Lowbury

I AM THE ONE

I am the one
who comes out
after dark.
My loveliness
rarer than
a black rose.
With me beauty
is not merely skin deep.
My eyes
pool of deep ocean waters
glittering under the sun.

To others
I am a ray
on a cold bleak day
Forever a daffodil
Penetrating as a needle
Brilliant as diamond.

I dine
with the moon and stars
allowing them to gaze
at my grace.

I am fragrant jasmine
innovative as the traffic light
Ancient as Timbuktu.

Yes, I am the one
Cool and protective
I'm a child of the night.

Opal Palmer Adisa

MAGIC STORY OF FALLING ASLEEP

When the last giant came out of his cave
and his bones turned into the mountain
and his clothes turned into the flowers,

nothing was left but his tooth
which my dad took home in his truck
which my granddad carved into a bed

which my mum tucks me into at night
when I dream of the last giant
when I fall asleep on the mountain

Nancy Willard

THE FIRST MUSIC

What was the first music
After the chirping of birds, the barking of foxes,
After the hoot of owls, the mooing of cows,
The murmur of dawn birds, winds in the trees?
Did all these tell the first men they must make
Their own music? Mothers would lullaby
Their babies to sleep, warriors certainly shouted.
But what was the first music that was its own
Purpose, a pattern or phrasing, a quality
Of sound that came between silences and cast out
All other possible sounds? It must have been man
Singing in love and exultation, hearing
The high sweet song of blackbirds. When did he fashion
A harp or horn? O how much I would give
To hear that first and pristine music and know
That it changed the turning planet and visited stars.

Elizabeth Jennings

STEELBAND DANCING

When dancing
in steelband
dohn hol han.
The way to move
you body,
deserves
serious study.

So lehme give
you some tips,
you mus swing
you hips
this way,
that way,
so an so
like
when you dance
calypso;

and
in road march
when steelband
sweet,
this is the way
to chip you feet.

John Lyons

529 1983

Absentmindedly,
sometimes,
I lift the receiver
And dial my own number

(What revelations,
I think then,
If only
I could get through to myself.)

Gerda Mayer

THE GREAT SPHINX BY THE NILE

A very strange creature indeed
is the Sphinx.
It stares in the sunlight,
and yet never blinx,
while day-trippers gaze
through the shimmering haze
with their cameras, sunhats,
and canned fizzy drinx.

Though no-one can ever know
what the Sphinx thinx,
it must feel relief
when the sun slowly sinx.
For then, with a smile,
off it trots to the Nile,
to the cool river bank
for a quick forty winx.

Barry Buckingham

OUCH!

Theophilus Thrapplethorn,
  The celebrated thistle-sifter,
While sifting a sieve of unsifted thistles,
  Thrust three thousand thistles
Through the thick of his thumb.
  If Theophilus Thrapplethorn
The successful thistle-sifter,
  Thrust three thousand thistles
Through the thick of his thumb,
  See that thou,
When thou siftest a sieve of thistles,
  Dost not get the unsifted thistles
Stuck in thy thumb!

Anonymous

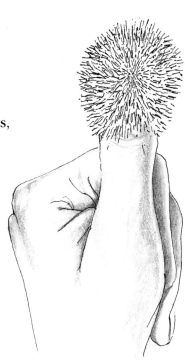

THE SONG OF THE HOMEWORKERS

Homework moanwork
Cross it out and groanwork
Homework neatwork
Keeps you off the streetwork
Homework moanwork
Cross it out and groanwork
Homework roughwork
When you've had enoughwork
Homework moanwork
Cross it out and groanwork
Homework dronework
Do it on your ownwork
Homework moanwork
Cross it out and groanwork

Homework gloomwork
Gaze around the roomwork
Homework moanwork
Cross it out and groanwork
Homework guesswork
Book is in a messwork
Homework moanwork
Cross it out and groanwork
Homework rushwork
Do it on the buswork
Homework moanwork
Cross it out and groanwork
Homework hatework
Hand your book in latework
Homework moanwork
Cross it out and groan groan GROANWORK

Trevor Millum

BE NICE TO RHUBARB

Please say a word for rhubarb,
    It hasn't many chums
For people like banana splits
    Or fancy juicy plums.

They slice the sweet, sweet melon
    Or gather tasty pears,
But if you mention rhubarb pie
    You get the rhudest stares.

They praise the yellow lemon,
    The golden orange cool,
But rhubarb's never mentioned
    Or that's the general rhule.

For rhubarb stewed and blushing
    I've only this to say,
If they should cast an unkind barb
    I'll see they rhu the day.

Max Fatchen

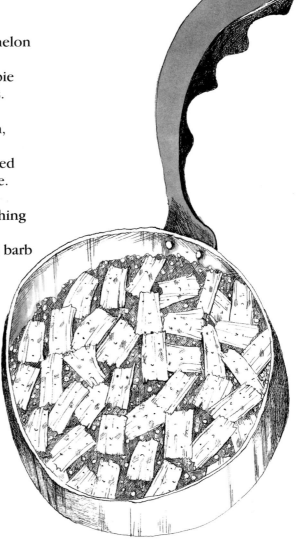

THE ENGLISH LANGUAGE

Some words have different meanings,
and yet they're spelt the same.
A cricket is an insect,
to play it - it's a game.
On every hand, in every land,
it's thoroughly agreed,
the English language to explain,
is very hard indeed.

Some people say that you're a dear,
yet dear is far from cheap.
A jumper is a thing you wear,
yet a jumper has to leap.
It's very clear, it's very queer,
and pray who is to blame
for different meanings to some words
pronounced and spelt the same?

A little journey is a trip,
a trip is when you fall.
It doesn't mean you have to dance
whene'er you hold a ball.
Now here's a thing that puzzles me:
musicians of good taste
will very often form a band -
I've one around my waist!

You spin a top, go for a spin,
or spin a yarn may be -
yet every spin's a different spin,
as you can plainly see.
Now here's a most peculiar thing,
'twas told me as a joke -
a dumb man wouldn't speak a word,
yet seized a wheel and spoke.

A door may often be ajar,
but give the door a slam,
and then your nerves receive a jar -
and then there's jars of jam.
You've heard, of course, of traffic jams,
and jams you give your thumbs.
And adders, too, one is a snake,
the other adds up sums.
A policeman is a copper,
it's a nickname (impolite!)
yet a copper in the kitchen
is an article you light.
On every hand, in every land,
it's thoroughly agreed -
the English language to explain
is very hard indeed!

Harry Hemsley

SURNAMES

Men once were surnamed for their shape or estate
   (You all may from history worm it),
There was Louis the bulky, and Henry the Great,
   John Lackland, and Peter the Hermit:
But now, when the doorplates of misters and dames
   Are read, each so constantly varies,
From the owner's trade figure, and calling surnames
   Seem given by the rule of contraries.

Mr. Wise is a dunce, Mr. King is a whig,
   Mr. Coffin's uncommonly sprightly,
And huge Mr. Little broke down in a gig
   While driving fat Mrs. Golightly.
At Bath, where the feeble go more than the stout
   (A conduct well worthy of Nero),
Over poor Mr. Lightfoot, confined with the gout,
   Mr. Heavyside danced a bolero.

Miss Joy, wretched maid, when she chose Mr. Love,
   Found nothing but sorrow await her;
She now holds in wedlock, as true as a dove,
   That fondest of mates, Mr. Hayter.
Mr. Oldcastle dwells in a modern-built hut;
   Miss Sage is of madcaps the archest;
Of all the queer bachelors Cupid e'er cut,
   Old Mr. Young hushand's starchest.

Mr. Child, in a passion, knock'd down Mr. Rock;
   Mr. Stone like an aspen-leaf shivers;
Miss Pool used to dance, but she stands like a stock
   Ever since she became Mrs. Rivers.
Mr. Swift hobbles onward, no mortal knows how,
   He moves as though cords had entwined him;
Mr. Metcalf ran off upon meeting a cow,
   With pale Mr. Turnbull behind him.

Mr. Barker's as mute as a fish in the sea,
    Mr. Miles never moves on a journey,
Mr. Gotobed sits up till half after three,
    Mr. Makepeace was bred an attorney,
Mr. Gardner can't tell a flower from a root,
    Mr. Wild with timidity draws back,
Mr. Ryder performs all his journeys on foot,
 Mr. Foot all his journeys on horseback.

Mr. Penny, whose father was rolling in wealth,
    Consumed all the fortune his dad won;
Large Mr. LeFever's the picture of health;
    Mr. Goodenough is but a bad one;
Mr. Cruikshank stept into three thousand a year
    By showing his leg to an heiress:
Now I hope you'll acknowledge I've made it quite clear
    Surnames ever go by contraries.

_____

James Smith

BAGGIN'

"G'up t' th' 'ouse 'n' get Baggin'…
'N' put wood in th' 'ole as y' go."
Well, not knowing what he said,
but not keen to be seen as daft
on my first job, I left him
Crouched under cows' udders,
And shut the milk shed door.

Stepping round the frosty yard,
slapping my arms against the chill,
I saw his wife at her window sill
in the vapours of a can of tea
and plates of melted-butter toast:
"Quick wi' thee, Lad," she scolded,
"'N' get this Baggin' out o' cold!"

So, as if I'd known all along
I received the steaming load,
then, swollen with duty, strode
down the yard to the feed-room,
where bales of hay and straw
were set, and men who'd worked
all morning sat, growling
"Baggin's 'ere. 'Bout time too!"

John Wright

WORDS ARE WAITING

Seek and you will find
Search and you will locate
Look and you will see
Hunt and you will track down

Chase and you will catch
Follow and you will meet
Pursue and you will stumble on
Trail and you will discover
Journey and you will arrive
Travel and you will get somewhere
Wander and you will encounter
Meander and you will bump into
Explore and you will find a way
Investigate and you will detect
Ask and you will be answered
Request and you will be granted
Enquire and you will find out
Question and you will be informed
Be curious and you will realize
Puzzle and you will solve
Probe and you will pinpoint the truth
Research and you will trace
Quest and you will retrieve
Delve and you will elicit
Dig and you will unearth
Excavate and you will uncover
Rummage and you will come upon
Examine and you will identify
Scrutinize and you will recognize
Consider and you will unfold
Test and you will perceive
Check and you will verify
Open your eyes and you will notice
Illuminate and you will see the light

Isn't this thesaurus wonderful?

Mike Jubb

HAVE YOU EVER THOUGHT ?

A comb has teeth but can't bite,
A shoe has a tongue but can't talk,
Rulers have feet and tables have legs
Yet neither of them can walk.

A chair has an arm but no elbow,
A clock has two hands but can't hold,
Hills have brows, and corn has ears
Though they never turn blue in the cold.

Needles and spuds have eyes
But not one of them can see,
And though a jug has a lip, and a tunnel a mouth,
They can't drink coffee or tea.

Rocks and clocks have faces,
Books have backs and a spine,
A well's got a bottom, a sausage a skin;
There's a neck on a bottle of wine.

Roads have hard shoulders but can't shrug,
A car has a body plus parts,
Tools have chests and chimneys have breasts.
But only people - and lettuces - have hearts!

Jacqueline Brown

RANT ABOUT PANTS

Some people call them knickers
My Granny calls them drawers
Hers used to keep the cold out
Now they're used for cleaning floors

Florists call them bloomers
And lawyers call them briefs
While undertakers solemnly say
A pair of underneaths

Fire fighters call them hosiery
Americans call them panties
Which are the nasty nylon kind
You get from distant aunties

Small people call them long johns
Tall people call them shorts
There's even combinations
Designed to fit all sorts

Lurking beneath a Scotsman's kilt
You're unlikely to find any
Which makes it nice and easy
When he wants to spend a penny

There are bikinis, teeny-weenies
Trunks with no frills or fuss
You should always wear a fresh pair
In case you're knocked down by a bus

There are hundreds of words for underwear
But I always call mine pants
They're white and clean and seldom seen
And they rhyme so well with ants

Lindsay Macrae

POETRY IS WHAT?

Poetry is a beautiful mud-pie
Washed down with a glassful of stars.

Poetry is one of the best ways
Of singing to the whole wide world
Or whispering in the ear of your best friend.

Poetry tunnels you out of your dungeon.
Poetry captures the three-headed dragon.
And teaches it Ludo and Frisbee-throwing.

Poetry is a Mammoth in a shopping mall,
A beggar with no legs in Disneyland,
A chocolate bicycle,
A truthburger with French flies
And the Moon's own telephone.

Poetry is your mind dancing
To the drumbeat of your heart.

Adrian Mitchell

ACCORDING TO MY MOOD

I have poetic licence, i WriTe thE way i waNt.
i drop my full stops where i like …
MY CAPITAL LeteRs go where i liKE,
i order from MY PeN, i verse the way i like (i do my spelling
    write)
Acording to my MOod.
i HAve poetic licence,
I put my comments where i like,,((( ))).
(((my brackets are write((
I REPEAT WHen i likE.

i can't go rong,
i look and i.c.
It's rite.
i REpeat when i liKE. i have
poetic licence!
Don't question me????

Benjamin Zephaniah

THE UNCERTAINTY OF THE POET

I am a poet
I am very fond of bananas.

I am bananas
I am very fond of a poet.

I am a poet of bananas.
I am very fond,

A fond poet of 'I am, I am' -
Very bananas,

Fond of 'Am I bananas,
Am I?' - a very poet.

Bananas of a poet!
Am I fond? Am I very?

Poet bananas! I am.
I am very fond of a 'very'.

I am of very fond bananas.
Am I a poet?

Wendy Cope

THE POET

The paper caught fire under his pen;
For a moment earth and sky were ablaze
And the light came from the paper.
But it burned; the sheet turned to ashes,
The fire went out.
And now when someone asks him
for a scrap of paper, he searches

Through pockets, drawers, and finds them empty.

Edward Lowbury

POETRY JUMP-UP

Tell me if ah seeing right
Take a look down de street

Words dancin
words dancin
till dey sweat
words like fishes
jumpin out a net
words wild and free
joinin de poetry revelry
words back to back
words belly to belly

Come on everybody
come and join de poetry band
dis is poetry carnival
dis is poetry bacchanal
when inspiration call
take yu pen in yu hand
if yu dont have a pen
take yu pencil in yu hand

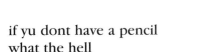
if yu dont have a pencil
what the hell
so long de feeling start to swell
just shout de poem out

Words jumpin off de page
tell me if Ah seeing right
words like birds
jumpin out a cage
take a look down de street
words shakin dey waist
words shakin dey bum
words wit black skin
words wit white skin
words wit brown skin
words wit no skin at all
words huggin up words
an sayin I want to be a poem today
rhyme or no rhyme
I is a poem today
I mean to have a good time

Words feelin hot hot hot
big words feelin hot hot hot
lil words feelin hot hot hot
even sad words cant help
tappin dey toe
to de riddum of de poetry band

Dis is poetry carnival
dis is poetry bacchanal
so come on everybody
join de celebration
all yu need is plenty perspiration
an a little inspiration
plenty perspiration
an a little inspiration

John Agard

THE DOZE

Through Dangly Woods the aimless Doze
A-dripping and a-dribbling goes.
His company no beast enjoys.
He makes a sort of hopeless noise
Between a snuffle and a snort.
His hair is neither long nor short;
His tail gets caught on briars and bushes,
As through the undergrowth he pushes.
His ears are big, but not much use.
He lives on blackberries and juice
And anything that he can get.
His feet are clumsy, wide and wet,
Slip-slopping through the bog and heather
All in the wild and weepy weather.
His young are many, and maltreat him;
But only hungry creatures eat him.
He pokes about in mossy holes,
Disturbing sleepless mice and moles,
And what he wants he never knows -
The damp, despised and aimless Doze.

James Reeves

JABBERWOCKY

'Twas brillig, and the slithy toves
    Did gyre and gimble in the wabe:
All mimsy were the borogoves,
    And the mome raths outgrabe.

'Beware the Jabberwock, my son!
    The jaws that bite, the claws that catch!
Beware the Jubjub bird, and shun
    The frumious Bandersnatch!'

He took his vorpal sword in hand:
    Long time the manxome foe he sought -
So rested he by the Tumtum tree,
    And stood awhile in thought.

And as in uffish thought he stood,
    The Jabberwock, with eyes of flame,
Came whiffling through the tulgey wood,
    And burbled as it came!

One, two! One, two! And through and through
    The vorpal blade went snicker-snack!
He left it dead, and with its head
    He went galumphing back.

'And hast thou slain the Jabberwock?
    Come to my arms, my beamish boy!
O frabjous day! Callooh! Callay!'
    He chortled in his joy.

'Twas brillig, and the slithy toves
    Did gyre and gimble in the wabe:
All mimsy were the borogoves,
    And the mome raths outgrabe.

Lewis Carroll

THE STATUE

In Parliament Square
there is the statue of a gentleman standing in front of
    a chair.
And all the time that the House of Commons is sitting,
ruling the country, outwitting
each other in the People's name,
some shouting 'Hear, Hear' and others 'Withdraw' or
    'Shame!'
this distinguished elderly person stands before an empty
    seat,
and every time I pass in the Number 29 bus, I greet
the great man and say with a worried frown:
'Aren't you tired, President Abraham Lincoln?
Why don't you sit down?'

_____

Edith Roseveare

THE VISIT

I thought I'd hid everything
that there wasnie wan
give away sign Left

I put Marx Engels Lenin (no Trotsky)
in the airing cupboard - she'll no be
checking out the towels surely

All the copies of the *Daily Worker*
I shoved under the sofa
the dove of peace I took down from the loo

A poster of Paul Robeson
saying give him his passport
I took down from the kitchen

I left a bust of Burns
my detective stories
and the *Complete Works of Shelley*

She comes at 11.30 exactly.
I pour her coffee
from my new Hungarian set

And foolishly prays she willnae
ask its origins - honestly
this baby is going to my head

She crosses her legs on the sofa
I fancy I hear the *Daily Workers*
rustle underneath her

Well she says, you have an interesting home
She sees my eyebrows rise
It's different she qualifies

Hell and I've spent all morning
trying to look ordinary
- a lovely home for the baby

She buttons her coat all smiles
I'm thinking
I'm on the home run

But just as we get to the last post
her eye catches at the same time as mine
a red ribbon with twenty world peace badges

Clear as a hammer and sickle
on the wall
oh she says are you against nuclear weapons?

To Hell with this. Baby or no baby.
Yes I says. Yes yes yes.
I'd like this baby to live in a nuclear free environment

Oh. Her eyes light up.
I'm all for peace myself she says
and sits down for another cup of coffee.

Jackie Kay

LANCE-CORPORAL DIXON

I saw a picture in the paper the other day
Of a soldier carrying a baby.
Lance-corporal Dixon was his name.
The baby?
His C.O.'s daughter.
My mother was touched by the picture,
Said it was charming
That a man so tough
Could be so gentle.
It looked odd to me:
A sten gun under one arm,
A baby under the other.

Linda Newton

SASSENACHS

Me and my best pal (well, she was
till a minute ago) - are off to London.
First trip on an inter-city alone.
When we got on we were the same
kind of excited - jigging on our seats,
staring at everyone. But then,
I remembered I was to be sophisticated.
So when Jenny starts shouting,
'Look at that the land's flat already'
when we are just outside Glasgow
(Motherwell actually) I feel myself flush.

Or even worse, 'Sassenach country!
Wey Hey Hey.' The tartan tammy
sitting proudly on top of her pony;

the tartan scarf swinging like a tail.
The nose pressed to the window.
'England's not so beautiful, is it?'
And we haven't even crossed the border!
And the train's jazzy beat joins her:
Sassenachs sassenachs here we come.
Sassenachs sassenachs Rum TumTum
Sassenachs sassenachs how do you do.
SASSENACHS SASSENACHS WE'LL GET YOU!

Then she loses momentum, so out come
the egg mayonnaise sandwiches and
the big bottle of bru. 'My ma's done us proud,'
says Jenny, digging in, munching loud.
The whole train is an egg and I'm inside it.
I try and remain calm; Jenny starts it again,
Sassenachs sassenachs Rum Tum Tum.

Finally we get there: London, Euston;
and the very first person on the platform
gets asked - 'are you a genuine sassenach?'
I want to die, but instead I say, 'Jenny!'
He replies in that English way -
'I beg your pardon,' and Jenny screams,
'Did you hear that Voice?'
And we both die laughing, clutching
our stomachs at Euston station.

Jackie Kay

BRENNAN ON THE MOOR

It's of a fearless highwayman a story I will tell,
His name was Willie Brennan and in Ireland he did dwell.
'Twas on the Kilworth mountains he began a wild career,
And many a noble gentleman before him shook with fear.

> Crying Brennan's on the moor! Brennan's on the moor!
> So bold and undaunted stood Bill Brennan on the moor.

'Twas on the King's own highway now Brennan he sat
    down,
He met the Mayor of Cashel just five miles out of town.
The Mayor he looked at Brennan and, 'I think now, boy,'
    says he,
'Your name is Billie Brennan; you must come along with
    me.'

Now Brennan's wife was going down town provisions for to
    buy,
And she seen Willie taken, ah sure she began to cry,
'Hand me ten pennies!' and sure just as he spoke,
She handed him a blunderbuss from underneath her cloak.

Brennan had his blunderbuss, my story I'll unfold,
He caused the Mayor of Cashel to deliver up his gold.
Five thousand pounds were offered for his apprehension
    there,
But Brennan and the pedlar to the mountain did repair.

Now Brennan is an outlaw upon a mountain high,
With Infantry and Cavalry to catch him they did try,
He laughed at them, he scorned at them until, it is said,
A false-hearted woman caused him to lose his head.

They hung him at the crossroads, in chains he swung and
     dried,
Some say in the midnight hour you still can see him ride.
You'll see him with his blunderbuss, and in the midnight
     chill
Along the King's own highway rides Willie Brennan still.

_____

Anonymous

DON'T

Don't comb your hair in company.
Don't cross the kitchen floor in welly boots.
Don't put the television on.
Don't squint. Don't get in fights.

Don't stuff your mouth with sausage.
Don't drop towels on the bathroom floor.
Don't hang about with that rough crowd.
Don't put your feet up on the chair.

Don't use up all the paper in the loo.
Don't scratch. Don't twitch. Don't sniff. Don't talk.
Don't stick your tongue out.
Don't you dare to answer back.

Life is full of opportunity, says my Mum.

_____

Barrie Wade

WHY DOROTHY WORDSWORTH IS NOT AS FAMOUS AS HER BROTHER

'I wandered lonely as a ...
They're in the top drawer, William,
Under your socks -
I wandered lonely as a -
No not that drawer, the top one.
I wandered by myself -
Well wear the ones you can find,
No, don't get overwrought my dear,
I'm coming.

'I was out one day wandering
Lonely as a cloud when -
Softboiled egg, yes my dear,
As usual, three minutes -
As a cloud when all of a sudden -
Look I said I'll cook it,
Just hold on will you -
All right. I'm coming.

'One day I was out for a walk
When I saw this flock -
It can't be too hard, it had three minutes.
Well put some butter in it.
This host of golden daffodils
As I was out for a stroll one -

'Oh you fancy a stroll, do you.
Yes, all right William. I'm coming.
It's on the peg. Under your hat.
I'll bring my pad, shall I, in case
You want to jot something down?'

Lynn Peters

THE RICHEST POOR MAN
IN THE VALLEY

On the outside
he seemed older than he was.
His face was like a weather map
full of bad weather
while inside
his heart was fat with sun.

With his two dogs
he cleared a thin silver path
across the Black Mountain.
And when winter
kicked in
they brought his sheep
down from the top
like sulky clouds.

Harry didn't care for things
that other people prize
like money, houses, bank accounts
and lies.
He was living in a caravan
until the day he died.

But at his funeral
his friends' tears
fell like a thousand
diamonds.

Lindsay MacRae

THE DILEMMAS OF AIDS

It's AIDS and I don't know what to do.
I've had it for years and I don't know what to do.
It gets worse and I don't know what to do.
I've had more advice from more quarters than I knew existed
And I don't know what to do.
People come to me and they say,
When they are honest,
They don't know what to do.
They ask
What can I do to help?
What can I tell them?
Some of them want to make commando raids on my psyche
And reveal in moments that which I've not discovered myself.
If I can't do it, I'm not being positive enough.
Not cooperating.

The professional carers have trained voices unless you ask for money.

The hospitals want to help -
They have to help -
Every fibre of their being is programmed to help.
They come across an illness they can't help.
Then like mad robots
They prod
And poke
And test
And slice.
And many times
They kill.

These views are not the views of a cynic,
But after these years they are the views of the sceptic.

Long ago and far away I wrote :

    Blood freed from the trapped body
    Washed across the floors of pain
    And sank into the head

Of the failed healer.

The healer cried
The body died
The blood just tried
To LIVE.

The worst of it is I understand why they all do this.
I understand.

But
I don't know what to do.

James Sykes

CONVERSATION WITH AN ANGEL

On my way to Sainsbury's
I met an Angel. He stood
relaxed, one foot and one wing
off the pavement, waiting
for me to pass. I stopped
to see if he needed anything: had he
lost his way? Could I help perhaps?
No, he lacked nothing, simply wanted
some contact with the world again;
he'd been human once and he sometimes
craved that bitter-sweet flavour …
Some angels were born - he explained -
others translated. Could I
become an angel? Was there a waiting list?
Not a chance for you, he laughed,
no one who has seen
an angel can ever become one.

Wanda Barford

TULLYNOE: TÊTE-A-TÊTE IN THE PARISH PRIEST'S PARLOUR

'Ah, he was a grand man.'
'He was: he fell out of the train going to Sligo.'
'He did: he thought he was going to the lavatory.'
'He did: in fact he stepped out of the rear door of the train.'
'He did: God, he must have got an awful fright.'
'He did: he saw that it was the railway tracks going away from him.'
'He did: I wonder if … but he was a grand man.'
'He was: he had the most expensive Toyota you can buy.'
'He had: well, it was only beautiful.'
'It was: he used to have an Audi.'
'He had: as a matter of fact he used to have two Audis.'
'He had: and then he had an Avenger.'
'He had: and then he had a Volvo.'
'He had: in the beginning he had a lot of Volkses.'
'He had: he was a great man for the Volkses.'
'He was: did he once have an Escort?'
'He had not: he had a son a doctor.'
'He had: and he had a Morris Minor too.'
'He had: he had a sister a hairdresser in Kilmallock.'
'He had: he had another sister a hairdresser in Ballybunion.'
'He had: he was put in a coffin which was put in his father's cart.'
'He was: his lady wife sat on top of the coffin driving the donkey.'
'She did: ah, but he was a grand man.'
'He was: he was a grand man … '
'Good night, Father.'
'Good night, Mary.'

Paul Durcan

I WISH I WERE

When the gong sounds at ten in the morning and I walk to school
    by our lane,
Every day I meet the hawker crying, 'Bangles, crystal bangles!'
There is nothing to hurry him on, there is no road he must take,
    no place he must go to, no time when he must come home.
I wish I were a hawker, spending my day in the road, crying,
    'Bangles, crystal bangles!'

When at four in the afternoon I come back from the school,
I can see through the gate of that house the gardener digging the
    ground.
He does what he likes with his spade, he soils his clothes with the
    dust,
Nobody takes him to task if he gets baked in the sun or gets wet.
I wish I were a gardener digging away at the garden with nobody
    to stop me from digging.

Just as it gets dark in the evening and my mother sends me to
    bed,
I can see through my open window the watchman walking up and
    down.
The lane is dark and lonely, and the street-lamp stands
Like a giant with one red eye in its head.

The watchman swings his lantern and walks with his shadow at
    his side, and never once goes to bed in his life.
I wish I were a watchman walking the streets all night, chasing
    the shadows with my lantern.

Rabindranath Tagore

SHOPPING

look over there in that window
isn't that lovely
the sort of thing that would
go with your hair
it would look nice on you

we'll go & try it on
shall we?
Well, all right; perhaps not
a bit saggy in the neck

well. What about this one?
i've told you before
i haven't got money to throw away
on rubbish
i don't like that
you know that kind of thing
looks terrible with your shoulders

you don't want that.
That's not what we're looking for.
you've several of those already.

What about this?
In another colour?
If they have it in your size.

i won't throw money away.
i've told you. No. no. no.
definitely not.
i don't care who else is wearing them

i can't understand
why you're so difficult
to please

Jenny Boult

HAIRCUT

What I hate
about having a haircut
is being asked
how I want it
when I don't want it cut at all.

What I hate
about having a haircut
is being asked
questions with
the whole room listening to my answers.

What I hate
about having a haircut
is being asked
to look in
the mirror and say how I like it.

What I hate most
about having a haircut
is going to school
and everyone
telling me I've had my hair cut.

Michael Harrison

DREAD-LOCK STYLE

Me don't want no hair style
cause me don't want no hair pile
pon me bedroom floor

I say me don't want no hair style
cause me don't want no hair pile
pon me bedroom floor

I think I gonna stick to me
dread-lock style
me dread-lock style
looking wild wild wild

dem hair gal
putting a dunno what on yuh hair
bunning up yuh scalp
thinking I was born yesterday

So I think I gonna stick
to me dread-lock style
me dread-lock style
looking wild wild wild

Lesley Miranda

THE FEET

At night, the feet become lonely.

All day they have considerable importance;
are carefully dressed in shoes
and ready at any moment to stand,
move around, take the weight of the body.
Even when the body is sitting, sometimes
the feet depress certain pedals
to control an automobile travelling at tremendous speeds
for hundreds of miles.

But at night
even their socks are taken away.
The feet are made to lie down naked
in a part of the bed no one visits.
All night they lie there, with nothing to do.

Hidden away in the darkness
under sheets and blankets
no wonder the two abandoned feet
begin a clumsy relationship.

One foot
suddenly crosses the ankle of the other
like a blind horse putting his head over the neck of another blind horse.
The feet lie like this, touching all night
- stiff, self-conscious, not saying a word.

Tom Wayman

DENTIST

What I hate
About going to the Dentist,
Is the waiting room,
Silent
Until someone screams behind a wall.

What I hate,
About going to the Dentist,
Is the smell of hygiene in the room,
And the chair squeaks as you sit down.

What I hate,
About going to the Dentist,
Is the chair moving,
Sounding like a factory,
And the blinding light, cast down in your eyes.

What I hate,
About going to the Dentist,
Is your mouth being stretched into an oblong,
The picking of the plaque,
And the scraping of teeth.

What I hate,
About going to the Dentist,
Is the drill that touches your teeth,
And makes your mouth shake,
Like a pneumatic drill on a road,
The vibrations like music on full blast.

What I hate,
About going to the Dentist,
Is the sharp injection of pain,
The hurt as the needle goes in,
That numbs your mouth,
That wobbles your tongue and lips,
Like jelly as you try to speak.

What I hate,
About going to the Dentist,
Is the slimy pink liquid,
The swallow and the spit.

What I like,
About going to the Dentist,
Is being given a sticker,
Being made a fuss of by Mum,
And watching my brother go in next!

Karina Bailey (Aged 9)

BREATHLESS

Written at 21000 feet on May 23rd 1953 climbing Everest

Heart aches,
Lungs pant
The dry air
Sorry, scant.
Legs lift
And why at all?
Loose drift,
Heavy fall.
Prod the snow
Its easiest way;
A flat step
Is holiday.
Look up,
The far stone
Is many miles
Far and alone.
Grind the breath
Once more and on;
Don't look up
Till journey's done.
Must look up,
Glasses are dim.

Wrench of hand
Is breathless limb.
Pause one step,
Breath swings back;
Swallow once,
Dry throat is slack.
Then on
To the far stone;
Don't look up,
Counts the steps done.
One step,
One heart-beat,
Stone no nearer
Dragging feet.
Heart aches,
Lungs pant
The dry air
Sorry, scant.

Wilfrid Noyce

EGG THOUGHTS

Soft-Boiled

I do not like the way you slide,
I do not like your soft inside,
I do not like you many ways,
And I could do for many days
Without a soft-boiled egg.

Sunny-Side-Up

With their yolks and whites all runny
They are looking at me funny.

Sunny-Side-Down

Lying face-down on the plate
On their stomachs there they wait.

Poached

Poached eggs on toast, why do you shiver
With such a funny little quiver?

Scrambled

I eat as well as I am able,
But some falls underneath the table.

Hard-Boiled

With so much suffering today
Why do them any other way?

Russell Hoban

THE PAWPAW

Four little boys, tattered,
Fingers and faces splattered
With mud, had climbed
In the rain and caught
A pawpaw which they brought,
Like a bomb, to my house. I saw
Them coming: a serious, mumbling,
Tumbling bunch who stopped
At the steps in a hunch.
Releasing the fruit from the leaf
it was wrapped in, I watched them
Carefully wash the pawpaw
Like a nugget of gold. This done,
With rainwater, till it shone
They climbed into the house
To present the present to me.
A mocking sign of the doom of all flesh?
Or the purest gold in the kingdom?

Edward Kamau Brathwaite

EVERYDAY THINGS

Millionaires, presidents - even kings
Can't get along without everyday things.

Were you president, king or millionaire,
You'd use a comb to comb your hair.

If you wished to be clean - and you would, I hope -
You'd take a bath with water and soap.

And you'd have to eat - if you wanted to eat -
Bread and vegetables, fish and meat;

While your drink for breakfast would probably be
Milk or chocolate, coffee or tea.

You'd have to wear - you could hardly refuse -
Under clothes, outer clothes, stockings and shoes.

If you wished to make a reminding note,
You'd take a pencil out of your coat;

And you couldn't sign a letter, I think
With anything better than pen and ink.

If you wanted to read, you'd be sure to look
At newspaper, magazine, or book;

And if it happened that you were ill,
You'd down some oil or choke on a pill.

If you had a cold I can only suppose
You'd use a handkerchief for your nose.

When you wanted to rest your weary head,
Like other folks, you'd hop into bed.

Millionaires, presidents - even kings
Can't get along without everyday things.

Jean Ayer

LEISURE

What is this life if, full of care,
We have no time to stand and stare?

No time to stand beneath the boughs
And stare as long as sheep or cows.

No time to see, when woods we pass,
Where squirrels hide their nuts in grass.

No time to see, in broad daylight,
Streams full of stars, like skies at night.

No time to turn at Beauty's glance,
And watch her feet, how they can dance.

No time to wait till her mouth can
Enrich that smile her eyes began.

A poor life this if, full of care,
We have no time to stand and stare.

W. H. Davies

MY TRUE LOVE

My true love hath my heart, and I have his,
  By just exchange, one for the other given
I hold his dear, and mine he cannot miss:
  There never was a better bargain driven.

His heart in me, keeps me and him in one,
  My heart in him, his thoughts and senses guides:
He loves my heart, for once it was his own:
  I cherish his, because in me it bides.

His heart his wound received from my sight:
  My heart was wounded, with his wounded heart,
For as from me, on him his hurt did light,
  So still methought in me his hurt did smart:
    Both equal hurt, in this change sought our bliss:
    My true love hath my heart and I have his.

Sir Philip Sidney

HE WISHES FOR THE CLOTHS OF HEAVEN

Had I the heavens' embroidered cloths,
Enwrought with golden and silver light,
The blue and the dim and the dark cloths
Of night and light and the half-light,
I would spread the cloths under your feet:
But I, being poor, have only my dreams;
I have spread my dreams under your feet;
Tread softly because you tread on my dreams.

William Butler Yeats

SONNET

I wish I could remember that first day,
First hour, first moment of your meeting me,
If bright or dim the season, it might be
Summer or Winter for aught I can say;
So unrecorded did it slip away,
So blind was I to see and to foresee,
So dull to mark the budding of my tree
That would not blossom yet for many a May.
If only I could recollect it, such
A day of days! I let it come and go
As traceless as a thaw of bygone snow;
It seemed to mean so little, meant so much;
If only now I could recall that touch,
First touch of hand in hand - Did one but know!

Christina Rossetti

My mistress' eyes are nothing like the sun;
Coral is far more red than her lips' red;
If snow be white, why then her breasts are dun;
If hairs be wires, black wires grow on her head.
I have seen roses damasked, red and white,
But no such roses, see I in her cheeks;
And in some perfumes is there more delight
Than in the breath that from my mistress reeks.
I love to hear her speak, yet well I know
That music hath a far more pleasing sound;
I grant I never saw a goddess go;
My mistress, when she walks, treads on the ground.
    And yet, by heaven, I think my love as rare
    As any she belied with false compare.

William Shakespeare

LOCHINVAR

O young Lochinvar is come out of the west,
Through all the wide Border his steed was the best;
And save his good broadsword he weapons had none,
He rode all unarm'd, and he rode all alone.
So faithful in love, and so dauntless in war,
There never was knight like young Lochinvar.

He staid not for brake, and he stopp'd not for stone,
He swam the Eske river where ford there was none;
But ere he alighted at Netherby gate,
The bride had consented, the gallant came late:
For a laggard in love, and a dastard in war,
Was to wed the fair Ellen of brave Lochinvar.

So boldly he enter'd the Netherby Hall,
Among bride's-men, and kinsmen, and brothers, and all:
Then spoke the bride's father, his hand on his sword,
(For the poor craven bridegroom said never a word,)
'O come ye in peace here, or come ye in war,
Or to dance at our bridal, young Lord Lochinvar?'

'I long woo'd your daughter, my suit you denied; -
Love swells like the Solway, but ebbs like its tide -
And now am I come, with this lost love of mine
To lead but one measure, drink one cup of wine.
There are maidens in Scotland more lovely by far,
That would gladly be bride to the young Lochinvar.'

The bride kiss'd the goblet: the knight took it up,
He quaff'd off the wine, and he threw down the cup.
She look'd down to blush, and she look'd up to sigh,
With a smile on her lips, and a tear in her eye.
He took her soft hand, ere her mother could bar, -
'Now tread we a measure!' said young Lochinvar.

So stately his form, and so lovely her face,
That never a hall such a galliard did grace;
While her mother did fret, and her father did fume,
And the bridegroom stood dangling his bonnet and plume;
And the bride-maidens whisper'd, "'Twere better by far
To have match'd our fair cousin with young Lochinvar.'

One touch to her hand, and one word in her ear,
When they reach'd the hall-door, and the charger stood near;
So light to the croupe the fair lady he swung,
So light to the saddle before her he sprung!
'She is won! we are gone, over bank, bush, and scaur;
They'll have fleet steeds that follow,' quoth young Lochinvar.

There was mounting 'mong Graemes of the Netherby clan;
Forsters, Fenwicks, and Musgraves, they rode and they ran:
There was racing and chasing on Cannobie Lee,
But the lost bride of Netherby ne'er did they see.
So daring in love, and so dauntless in war,
Have ye e'er heard of gallant like young Lochinvar?

Sir Walter Scott

GROWING PAIN

The boy was barely five years old.
We sent him to the little school
And left him there to learn the names
Of flowers in jam jars on the sill
And learn to do as he was told.
He seemed quite happy there until
Three weeks afterwards, at night,
The darkness whimpered in his room.
I went upstairs, switched on his light,
And found him wide awake, distraught,
Sheets mangled and his eiderdown
Untidy carpet on the floor.
I said, 'Why can't you sleep? A pain?'
He snuffled, gave a little moan,
And then he spoke a single word:
'Jessica.' The sound was blurred.
'Jessica? What do you mean?'
'A girl at school called Jessica,
She hurts -'' he touched himself between
The heart and stomach ' - she has been
Aching here and I can see her.'
Nothing I had read or heard
Instructed me in what to do.
I covered him and stroked his head.
'The pain will go, in time,' I said.

Vernon Scannell

FIRST KISS

My problem is
I don't know how
to kiss.

What happens
to your teeth?

Will our lips stick?

Should you blow?

What if I spit
and dribble?

I'd like to
but hope
I don't giggle ...

I might
just decide
to say no though.

Joan Poulson

THE LADY OF SHALOTT

Part One

On either side the river lie
Long fields of barley and of rye,
That clothe the wold and meet the sky;
And thro' the field the road runs by
    To many-tower'd Camelot;
And up and down the people go,
Gazing where the lilies blow
Round an island there below,
    The island of Shalott.

Willows whiten, aspens quiver,
Little breezes dusk and shiver
Thro' the wave that runs for ever
By the island in the river
    Flowing down to Camelot.
Four grey walls, and four grey towers,
Overlook a space of flowers,
And the silent isle imbowers
    The Lady of Shalott.

By the margin, willow-veil'd,
Slide the heavy barges trail'd
By slow horses; and unhail'd
The shallop flitteth silken-sail'd
    Skimming down to Camelot:
But who hath seen her wave her hand?
Or at the casement seen her stand?
Or is she known in all the land,
    The Lady of Shalott?

Only reapers, reaping early
In among the bearded barley,
Hear a song that echoes cheerly
From the river winding clearly,
        Down to tower'd Camelot:
And by the moon the reaper weary,
Piling sheaves in uplands airy,
Listening, whispers "'Tis the fairy
        Lady of Shalott."

Part Two

There she weaves by night and day
A magic web with colours gay.
She has heard a whisper say,
A curse is on her if she stay
        To look down to Camelot.
She knows not what the curse may be,
And so she weaveth steadily,
And little other care hath she,
        The Lady of Shalott.

And moving thro' a mirror clear
That hangs before her all the year,
Shadows of the world appear.
There she sees the highway near
        Winding down to Camelot.
There the river eddy whirls,
And there the surly village-churls,
And the red cloaks of market girls,
        Pass onward from Shalott.

Sometimes a troop of damsels glad,
An abbot on an ambling pad,
Sometimes a curly shepherd-lad,
Or long-hair'd page in crimson clad,
    Goes by to tower'd Camelot;
And sometimes thro' the mirror blue
The knights come riding two and two:
She hath no loyal knight and true,
    The Lady of Shalott.

But in her web she still delights
To weave the mirror's magic sights,
For often thro' the silent nights
A funeral, with plumes and lights,
    And music, went to Camelot:
Or when the moon was overhead,
Came two young lovers lately wed;
"I am half sick of shadows," said
    The Lady of Shalott.

Part Three

A bow-shot from her bower-eaves,
He rode between the barley-sheaves,
The sun came dazzling thro' the leaves,
And flamed upon the brazen greaves
    Of bold Sir Lancelot.
A red-cross knight for ever kneel'd
To a lady in his shield,
That sparkled on the yellow field,
    Beside remote Shalott.

The gemmy bridle glitter'd free,
Like to some branch of stars we see
Hung in the golden Galaxy.
The bridle bells rang merrily

As he rode down to Camelot:
And from his blazon'd baldric slung
A mightly silver bugle hung,
And as he rode his armour rung,
    Beside remote Shalott.

All in the blue unclouded weather
Thick-jewell'd shone the saddle-leather,
The helmet and the helmet-feather
Burn'd like one burning flame together,
    As he rode down to Camelot.
As often thro' the purple night,
Below the starry clusters bright,
Some bearded meteor, trailing light,
    Moves over still Shalott.

His broad clear brow in sunlight flow'd;
On burnish'd hooves his war-horse trode;
From underneath his helmet flow'd
His coal-black curls as on he rode,
    As he rode down to Camelot.
From the bank and from the river
He flash'd into the crystal mirror,
"Tirra lirra," by the river
    Sang Sir Lancelot.

She left the web, she left the loom,
She made three paces thro' the room,
She saw the water-lily bloom,
She saw the helmet and the plume,
    She look'd down to Camelot.
Out flew the web and floated wide,
The mirror crack'd from side to side;
"The curse is come upon me!" cried
    The Lady of Shalott.

Part Four

In the stormy east-wind straining,
The pale yellow woods were waning,
The broad stream in his banks complaining,
Heavily the low sky raining
     Over tower'd Camelot;
Down she came and found a boat
Beneath a willow left afloat,
And round about the prow she wrote
    The Lady of Shalott.

And down the river's dim expanse -
Like some bold seer in a trance,
Seeing all his own mischance -
With a glassy countenance
    Did she look to Camelot.
And at the closing of the day
She loosed the chain, and down she lay;
The broad stream bore her far away,
    The Lady of Shalott.

Lying, robed in snowy white
That loosely flew to left and right -
The leaves upon her falling light -
Thro' the noises of the night
    She floated down to Camelot:
And as the boat-head wound along
The willowy hills and fields among,
They heard her singing her last song,
    The Lady of Shalott.

Heard a carol, mournful, holy,
Chanted loudly, chanted lowly,
Till her blood was frozen slowly,
And her eyes were darken'd wholly,
      Turn'd to tower'd Camelot;
For ere she reach'd upon the tide
The first house by the water-side,
Singing in her song she died.
      The Lady of Shalott.

Under tower and balcony,
By garden-wall and gallery,
A gleaming shape she floated by,
Dead-pale between the houses high,
      Silent into Camelot.
Out upon the wharfs they came,
Knight and burgher, lord and dame,
And round the prow they read her name,
      The Lady of Shalott.

Who is this? and what is here?
And in the lighted palace near
Died the sound of royal cheer;
And they cross'd themselves for fear,
      All the knights at Camelot:
But Lancelot mused a little space;
He said, "She has a lovely face;
God in His mercy lend her grace,
      The Lady of Shalott."

Alfred, Lord Tennyson

WHAT MY LADY DID

I asked my lady what she did
　　She gave me a silver flute and smiled.
A musician I guessed, yes that would explain
　　Her temperament so wild.

I asked my lady what she did
　　She gave me a comb inlaid with pearl.
A hairdresser I guessed, yes that would explain
　　Each soft and billowing curl.

I asked my lady what she did
　　She gave me a skein of wool and left.
A weaver I guessed, yes that would explain
　　Her fingers long and deft.

I asked my lady what she did
　　She gave me a slipper trimmed with lace.
A dancer I guessed, yes that would explain
　　Her suppleness and grace.

I asked my lady what she did
　　She gave me a picture not yet dry.
A painter I guessed, yes that would explain
　　The steadiness of her eye.

I asked my lady what she did
　　She gave me a fountain pen of gold.
A poet I guessed, yes that would explain
　　The strange stories that she told.

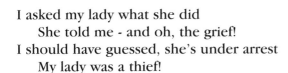

I asked my lady what she did
    She told me - and oh, the grief!
I should have guessed, she's under arrest
    My lady was a thief!

Roger McGough

ON A PAINTED WOMAN

To youths, who hurry thus away,
How silly your desire is -
At such an early hour to pay
Your compliments to Iris.

Stop, prithee, stop, ye hasty beaux,
No longer urge this race on;
Though Iris has put on her clothes,
She has not put her face on.

Percy Bysshe Shelley

DOWN IN THE VALLEY

Down in the valley, valley so low,
Hang your head over, hear the wind blow.
    Hear the wind blow, love, hear the wind blow,
    Hang your head over, hear the wind blow.

If you don't love me, love whom you please,
But throw your arms round me, give my heart ease.
    Give my heart ease, dear, give my heart ease.
    Throw your arms round me, give my heart ease.

Down in the valley, walking between,
Telling our story, here's what it sings:
    Here's what it sings, dear, here's what it sings,
    Telling our story, here's what it sings:

Roses of sunshine, vi'lets of dew,
Angels in heaven knows I love you,
    Knows I love you, dear, knows I love you,
    Angels in heaven knows I love you.

Build me a castle forty feet high,
So I can see her as she goes by,
    As she goes by, dear, as she goes by,
    So I can see her as she goes by.

Bird in a cage, love, bird in a cage,
Dying for freedom, ever a slave;
    Ever a slave, dear, ever a slave,
    Dying for freedom, ever a slave.

Write me a letter, send it by mail,
And back it in care of the Birmingham jail.
    Birmingham jail, love, Birmingham jail,
    And back it in care of the Birmingham jail.

American Spiritual

IT ISN'T THE SAME

Just one more song and then I'll get up
It's cold here and this bed offers little warmth
More than can be said of this room
In February in Yorkshire without you.

The snow we had last month is still on the moors
I can see it from the kitchen window
The wind lets me know it's there each morning
And the clouds stop the sun and me from smiling.

Why don't you come back home?
Why am I sitting here each night listening to next door's TV
Through paper thin walls and thinking of you
Nothing is the same now you've left.

I got my letters back all returned un-opened
At least you haven't forgotten our address
Did I really send so many?
I re-read them all and nurse my head.

Your brother came by to pick up your things
On his way back from college
He said you were fine and working in Kent
Where exactly is Kent, and where exactly are you?

I gave him another letter putting everything straight
That I love you and I want to be with you
He looked at me as he drove away and smiled
Maybe one day you will smile for me again.

---

m.m.s.

SANDWRITING

Scrawled in the wet sand
At low tide: 'STEVE LOVES
HILARY FOREVER.'
Like an epitaph for a grave
Still to be dug, the message
Shares with love itself
A disbelief in Time.

Time doesn't count for much
With Steve's brow unwrinkled
And Hilary's cheek porcelain;
'Forever' means a permanent 'Now';
the clock repeats itself
From day to day, and smiles
In friendly collusion.

But this wet sand is covered
With tiny wrinkles; rising
Water covers dreams, castles;
And a now unsmiling clock
Has something new to say:
'Forever' means 'Until
The next high tide.'

Edward Lowbury

WHEN LOVE IS DONE

The night has a thousand eyes,
    And the day but one;
Yet the light of the bright world dies
    With the dying sun.

The mind has a thousand eyes,
    And the heart but one;
Yet the light of a whole life dies
    When love is done.

Francis William Bourdillon

JENNY KISSED ME

Jenny kissed me when we met,
   Jumping from the chair she sat in;
Time, you thief, who love to get
   Sweets into your list, put that in!
Say I'm weary, say I'm sad,
   Say that health and wealth have missed me,
Say I'm growing old, but add,
   Jenny kissed me.

Leigh Hunt

I HAVE LIVED AND I HAVE LOVED

I have lived and I have loved;
I have waked and I have slept;
I have sung and I have danced;
I have smiled and I have wept;
I have won and wasted treasure;
I have had my fill of pleasure;
And all these things were weariness,
And some of them were dreariness.
And all of these things - but two things
Were emptiness and pain:
And Love - it was the best of them:
And Sleep - worth all the rest of them.

———————
Anonymous

THE HOST OF THE AIR

O'Driscoll drove with a song
The wild duck and the drake
From the tall and the tufted reeds
Of the drear Hart Lake.

And he saw how the reeds grew dark
At the coming of night-tide,
And dreamed of the long dim hair
Of Bridget his bride.

He heard while he sang and dreamed
A piper piping away,
And never was piping so sad,
And never was piping so gay.

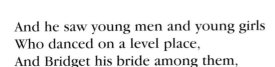

And he saw young men and young girls
Who danced on a level place,
And Bridget his bride among them,
With a sad and gay face.

The dancers crowded about him
And many a sweet thing said,
And a young man brought him red wine
And a young girl white bread.

But Bridget drew him by the sleeve
Away from the merry bands,
To old men playing at cards
With a twinkling of ancient hands.

The bread and the wine had a doom.
For these were the host of the air;
He sat and played in a dream
Of her long dim hair.

He played with the merry old men
And thought not of evil chance,
Until one bore Bridget his bride
Away from the merry dance.

He bore her away in his arms,
The handsomest young man there,
And his neck and his breast and his arms
Were drowned in her long dim hair.

O'Driscoll scattered the cards
And out of his dream awoke:
Old men and young men and young girls
Were gone like a drifting smoke;

But he heard high up in the air
A piper piping away,
And never was piping so sad,
And never was piping so gay.

William Butler Yeats

THE DEATH OF ROMEO AND JULIET

Romeo rode to the sepulchre, 'mong dead folks, bats, and
    creepers;
And swallowed down the burning dose - when Juliet oped
    her peepers.
'Are you alive? Or is't your ghost? Speak quick, before I go.'
'Alive! she cried, 'and kicking too; art thou my Romeo?'
'It is your Romeo, my faded little blossom;
O Juliet! is it possible that you were acting possum?'
'I was indeed; now let's go home; pa's spite will have abated;
What ails you love, you stagger so; are you intoxicated?'
'No, no, my duck; I took some stuff that caused a little fit;'
He struggled hard to tell her all, but couldn't, so he quit.
In shorter time than't takes a lamb to wag his tail, or jump
Poor Romeo was stiff and pale as any whitewashed pump.
Then Juliet seized that awful knife, and in her bosom stuck it,
Let out a most terrific yell, fell down, and kicked the bucket.

Anonymous

SHE DWELT AMONG
THE UNTRODDEN WAYS

She dwelt among the untrodden ways
    Beside the springs of Dove,
A Maid whom there were none to praise
    And very few to love:

A violet by a mossy stone
    Half hidden from the eye!
Fair as a star, when only one
    Is shining in the sky.

She lived unknown, and few could know
    When Lucy ceased to be;
But she is in her grave, and, oh,
    The difference to me!

William Wordsworth

Time is too slow for those who wait,
too swift for those who fear,
too long for those who grieve,
too short for those who rejoice,
but for those who love, time is eternity.

Anonymous

THREE FISHERS WENT SAILING

Three fishers went sailing out into the West,
    Away to the West as the sun went down;
Each thought on the woman who loved him the best,
    And the children stood watching them out of the town:
For men must work, and women must weep,
And there's little to earn, and many to keep,
    Though the harbour-bar be moaning.

Three wives sat up in the lighthouse tower,
    And they trimm'd the lamps as the sun went down;
And they looked at the squall, and they looked at the shower,
    And the night-rack came rolling up ragged and brown;
But men must work, and women must weep,
Though storms be sudden, and waters deep,
    And the harbour-bar be moaning.

Three corpses lay out on the shining sands,
    In the morning gleam, as the tide went down,
And the women are weeping and wringing their hands,
    For those who will never come home to the town.
For men must work, and women must weep,
And the sooner it's over, the sooner to sleep,
    And good-bye to the bar and its moaning.

Charles Kingsley

THE ALICE JEAN

One moonlight night a ship drove in,
    A ghost ship from the west,
Drifting with bare mast and lone tiller;
    Like a mermaid drest
In long green weed and barnacles
    She beached and came to rest.

All the watchers of the coast
    Flocked to view the sight;
Men and women, streaming down
    Through the summer night,
Found her standing tall and ragged
    Beached in the moonlight.

Then one old woman stared aghast:
    'The Alice Jean? But no!
The ship that took my Ned from me
    Sixty years ago -
Drifted back from the utmost west
    With the ocean's flow?

'Caught and caged in the weedy pool
    Beyond the western brink,
Where crewless vessels lie and rot
    In waters black as ink,
Torn out at last by a sudden gale -
    Is it the Jean, you think?'

A hundred women gaped at her,
    The menfolk nudged and laughed,
But none could find a likelier story
    For the strange craft
With fear and death and desolation
    Rigged fore and aft.

The blind ship came forgotten home
    To all but one of these,
Of whom none dared to climb aboard her:
    And by and by the breeze
Veered hard about, and the Alice Jean
    Foundered in the foaming seas.

Robert Graves

THE PRESS-GANG

Here's the tender coming,
  Pressing all the man;
    O, dear honey,
  What shall we do then?
Here's the tender coming,
  Off at Shields Bar.
Here's the tender coming,
  Full of men of war.

Here's the tender coming,
  Stealing of my dear;
    O, dear honey,
They'll ship you out of here,
  They'll ship you foreign,
For that is what it means.
Here's the tender coming,
Full of red marines.

Anonymous

CARGOES

Quinquireme of Nineveh from distant Ophir
Rowing home to haven in sunny Palestine,
With a cargo of ivory,
And apes and peacocks,
Sandalwood, cedarwood, and sweet white wine.

Stately Spanish galleon coming from the Isthmus,
Dipping through the Tropics by the palm-green shores,
With a cargo of diamonds,
Emeralds, amethysts,
Topazes, and cinnamon, and gold moidores.

Dirty British coaster with a salt-caked smoke stack
Butting through the Channel in the mad March days,
With a cargo of Tyne coal,
Road-rail, pig-lead
Firewood, iron-ware, and cheap tin trays.

John Masefield

STORM AT SEA

Sometimes I plunge through the press of the waves
Unexpectedly, delving to the earth,
The ocean bed. The waters ferment,
Sea-horses foaming.
The whale-mere roars, fiercely rages,
Waves beat upon the shore; stones and sand,
Seaweed and saltspray, are savagely flung
Against the dunes when, wrestling
Far beneath the waves, I disturb the earth,
The vast depths of the sea. Nor can I escape
My ocean bed before he permits me who is my pilot
On every journey. Tell me, wise man:
Who separates me from the sea's embrace,
When the waters become quiet once more,
The waves calm which before had covered me?

Kevin Crossley-Holland

MARY CELESTE

Only the wind sings
in the riggings,
the hull creaks a lullaby;
a sail lifts gently
like a message
pinned to a vacant sky.
The wheel turns
over bare decks,
shirts flap on a line;
only the song of the lapping waves
beats steady time ...

First mate,
off-duty from
the long dawn watch, begins
a letter to his wife, daydreams
of home.

The Captain's wife is late;
the child did not sleep
and breakfast has passed ...
She, too, is missing home;
sits down at last to eat,
but can't quite force
the porridge down.
She swallows hard,
slices the top from her egg.

The second mate
is happy.
A four-hour sleep,
full stomach
and a quiet sea
are all he craves.
He has all three.

Shirts washed and hung, beds
made below, decks done, the boy
stitches a torn sail.

The Captain
has a good ear for a tune;
played his child to sleep
on the ship's organ.
Now, music left,
he checks his compass,
lightly tips the wheel,
hopes for a westerly.
Clear sky, a friendly sea,
fair winds for Italy.

The child now sleeps, at last,
head firmly pressed into her pillow
in a deep sea-dream.

Then why are the gulls wheeling
like vultures in the sky?
Why was the child snatched
from her sleep? What drew
The Captain's cry?

Only the wind replies
in the rigging,
and the hull creaks and sighs;
a sail spells out its message
over silent skies.
The wheel still turns
over bare decks,
shirts blow on the line;
the siren-song of lapping waves
still echoes over time.

Judith Nicholls

UNCLE RODERICK

His drifter swung in the night
from a mile of nets
between the Shiants and Harris.

My boy's eyes watched
the lights of the fishing fleet - fireflies
on the green field of the sea.

In the foc's'le he gave me a bowl
of tea, black, strong and bitter,
and a biscuit you hammered
in bits like a plate.

The fiery curtain came up
from the blackness, comma'd with corpses.

Round Rhu nan Cuideagan
he steered for home, a boy's god
in seaboots. He found his anchorage
as a bird its nest.

In the kitchen he dropped
his oilskins where he stood.

He was strong as the red bull.
He moved like a dancer.
He was a cran of songs.

Norman MacCaig

SAILOR

He sat upon the rolling deck
Half a world away from home,
And smoked a Capstan cigarette
And watched the blue waves tipped with foam.

He had a mermaid on his arm,
An anchor on his breast,
And tattooed on his back he had
A blue bird in a nest.

Langston Hughes

PARTING AT MORNING

Round the cape of a sudden came the sea,
And the sun looked over the mountain's rim -
And straight was a path of gold for him,
And the need of a world of men for me.

Robert Browning

O Lord! Methought what pain it was to drown,
What dreadful noise of waters in my ears,
What sights of ugly death within my eyes.
Methought I saw a thousand fearful wrecks,
Ten thousand men that fishes gnawed upon,
Wedges of gold, great ouches, heaps of pearls,
Inestimable stones, unvalued jewels,
All scattered in the bottom of the sea.
Some lay in dead men's skulls; and in those holes
Where eyes did once inhabit, there were crept -
As 'twere in scorn of eyes - reflecting gems,
Which wooed the slimy bottom of the deep
And mocked the dead bones that lay scattered by.

William Shakespeare   *from Richard III*

SOUVENIR FROM WESTON-SUPER-MARE

Moving in a bunch like creeping hands
    the donkeys, prised from their hay,
cross the day's backdrop again; cloud, tide, mud
    cement the scene grey.

I scoop away. I build. I mould - the oil's
    good for adhesion. There, that
can do for the necessary moat,
    and look! A sand-cat!

Ears, nose, paws straight from Egypt. And still
    ten minutes before the bus.
We look back from the top of the wall.
    Long drawn out after us

a family comes breasting the wind -
it'll be right in their track.
The boy spots it first, running ahead.
    He goes running back

to fetch the others. They cluster and point,
    looking up and down the strand
before the wind detaches them again.
    He waits. Their backs turned,

he drops to his knees, he strokes the sand fur.
    Come on - five past the bus leaves!
Dodging the weaving cars we race the station
    clock's hands light as thieves.

Libby Houston

THE FRINGE OF THE SEA

We do not like to awaken
far from the fringe of the sea,
we who live upon small islands.

We like to rise up early,
quick in the agile mornings
and walk out only little distances
to look down at the water,

to know it is swaying near to us
with songs, and tides, and endless boatways,
and undulate patterns and moods.

We want to be able to saunter beside it
slowpaced in burning sunlight,
barearmed, barefoot, bareheaded,

and to stoop down by the shallows
sifting the random water
between assaying fingers
like farmers do with soil,

and to think of turquoise mackerel
turning with consummate grace,
sleek and decorous
and elegant in high blue chambers.

We want to be able to walk out into it,
to work in it,
dive and swim and play in it,

to row and sail
and pilot over its sandless highways,
and to hear
its call and murmurs wherever we may be.

All who have lived upon small islands
want to sleep and awaken
close to the fringe of the sea.

A L Hendriks

CHRISTMAS AT SEA

The sheets were frozen hard, and they cut the naked hand;
The decks were like a slide, where a seaman scarce could stand;
The wind was a nor'wester, blowing squally off the sea;
And cliffs and spouting breakers were the only things a-lee.

They heard the surf a-roaring before the break of day;
But 'twas only with the peep of light we saw how ill we lay.
We tumbled every hand on deck instanter, with a shout,
And we gave her the maintops'l, and stood by to go about.

All day we tacked and tacked between the South Head and the North;
All day we hauled the frozen sheets, and got no further forth;
All day as cold as charity, in bitter pain and dread,
For very life and nature we tacked from head to head.

We gave the South a wider berth, for there the tide-race roared;
But every tack we made we brought the North Head close aboard:
So's we saw the cliffs and houses, and the breakers running high,
And the coastguard in his garden, with his glass against his eye.

The frost was on the village roofs as white as ocean foam;
The good red fires were burning bright in every 'longshore home;
The windows sparkled clear, and the chimneys volleyed out;
And I vow we sniffed the vituals as the vessel went about.

The bells upon the church were rung with a mighty jovial cheer
For it's just that I should tell you how (of all days in the year)
This day of our adversity was blessed Christmas morn,
And the house above the coastguard's was the house where I was born.

O well I saw the pleasant room, the pleasant faces there,
My mother's silver spectacles, my father's silver hair;
And well I saw the firelight, like a flight of homely elves,
Go dancing round the china-plates that stand upon the shelves.

And well I knew the talk they had, the talk that was of me,
Of the shadow on the household and the son that went to sea;
And O the wicked fool I seemed, in every kind of way,
To be here and hauling frozen ropes on blessed Christmas Day.

They lit the high sea-light, and the dark began to fall.
"All hands to loose topgallant sails," I heard the captain call,
"By the Lord, she'll never stand it," our first mate, Jackson, cried.
... "It's the one way or the other, Mr. Jackson," he replied.

She staggered to her bearings, but the sails were new and good.
And the ship smelt up to windward just as though she understood.
As the winter's day was ending, in the entry of the night,
We cleared the weary headland, and passed below the light.

And they heaved a mighty breath, every soul on board but me,
As they saw her nose again pointing handsome out to sea;
But all that I could think of, in the darkness and the cold,
Was just that I was leaving home and my folks were growing old.

Robert Louis Stevenson

TALKING TURKEYS!!

Be nice to yu turkeys dis christmas
Cos turkeys jus wanna hav fun
Turkeys are cool, turkeys are wicked
An every turkey has a Mum.
Be nice to yu turkeys dis christmas,
Don't eat it, keep it alive,
It could be yu mate an not on yu plate
Say, Yo! Turkey I'm on your side.

I got lots of friends who are turkeys
An all of dem fear christmas time,
Dey wanna enjoy it, dey say humans destroyed it
An humans are out of dere mind,
Yeah, I got lots of friends who are turkeys
Dey all hav a right to a life,
Not to be caged up an genetically made up
By any farmer an his wife.

Turkeys jus wanna play reggae
Turkeys jus wanna hip-hop
Can you imagine a nice young turkey saying,
'I cannot wait for de chop?'
Turkeys like getting presents, dey wanna watch christmas TV,
Turkeys hav brains an turkeys feel pain
In many ways like yu an me.

I once knew a turkey called Turkey
He said 'Benji explain to me please,
Who put de turkey in christmas
An what happens to christmas trees?'
I said, 'I am not too sure turkey
But it's nothing to do wid Christ Mass
Humans get greedy an waste more dan need be
An business men mek loadsa cash.'

Be nice to yu turkey dis christmas
Invite dem indoors fe sum greens
Let dem eat cake an let dem partake
In a plate of organic grown beans,
Be nice to yu turkey dis christmas
An spare dem de cut of de knife,
Join Turkeys United an dey'll be delighted
An yu will mek new friends 'FOR LIFE'.

Benjamin Zephaniah

PREPARATIONS

Yet if His Majesty, our sovereign lord,
Should of his own accord
Friendly himself invite
And say, 'I'll be your guest tomorrow night,'
How should we stir ourselves, call and command
All hands to work! 'Let no man idle stand!
Set me fine Spanish tables in the hall;
See they be fitted all;
Let there be room to eat,
And order taken that there want no meat.
See every sconce and candlestick made bright,
That without tapers they may give a light.
Look to the presence: are the carpets spread,
The dazie o'er head,
The cushions in the chairs,
And all the candles lighted on the stairs?
Perfume the chambers, and in any case
Let each man give attendance in his place!

Thus, if a king were coming, would we do;
And 'twere good reason too;
For 'tis a duteous thing
To show all honour to an earthly king,
And after all our travail and our cost,
So he be pleased, to think no labour lost.
But at the coming of the King of Heaven
All's set at six and seven;
We wallow in our sin,
Christ cannot find a chamber in the inn.
We entertain Him always like a stranger,
And, as at first, still lodge Him in the manger.

Anonymous

CHRISTMAS DAYBREAK

Before the paling of the stars,
Before the winter morn,
Before the earliest cockcrow,
Jesus Christ was born:
Born in a stable,
Cradled in a manger,
In the world His hands had made,
Born a stranger.

Priest and king lay fast asleep
In Jerusalem,
Young and old lay fast asleep
in crowded Bethlehem:
Saint and angel, ox and ass,
Kept a watch together,
Before the Christmas daybreak
In the winter weather.

Jesus on His Mother's breast
In the stable cold,
Spotless Lamb of God was He,
Shepherd of the fold.
Let us kneel with Mary Maid,
With Joseph bent and hoary,
With saint and angel, ox and ass,
To hail the King of Glory.

Christina Rossetti

THE DONKEY'S CHRISTMAS

Plodding on,
From inn to inn,
No room to spare,
No room but a stable bare.
We rest,
And the following morning Jesus is born.
I gaze on the wondrous sight.
The King is born,
The King in a stable.
I see great lights,
Lights that are angels.
Everyone comes to see this sight.
I carried Mary,
Holy Mary,
Last night.

Anonymous

AFRICAN CHRISTMAS

Here are no signs of festival,
No holly and no mistletoe,
No robin and no crackling fire,
And no soft, feathery fall of snow.

In England one could read the words
Telling how shepherds in the fold
Followed the star and reached the barn
Which kept the Saviour from the cold,

And picture in one's mind the scene -
The tipsy, cheerful foreign troops,
The kindly villagers who stood
About the Child in awkward groups.

But in this blazing Christmas heat
The ox, the ass, the bed of hay
The shepherds and the Holy Child
Are stilted figures in a play.

Exiles, we see that we, like slaves
To symbol and to memory,
Have worshipped, not the
incarnate Christ,
But tinsel on the
Christmas tree.

John Press

I'M NOT OLD ENOUGH YET

Even at three, this business of a big man
coming down the chimney loaded with pressies
from your list (who showed it to him?
Why wasn't he covered in soot?) seemed a bit far-fetched.
Especially since we didn't have a chimney.
But later I started to believe in this man
with the beard longer than God's.
I left food out. I tried to stay awake.
I still suspected Santa was a black woman dressed in red,
but I never, since three, asked my mum any questions.
Now I'm seven. A pal of mine asks, 'Do you believe
in Santa Claus?' *What do you mean?* 'Do you think it's true,'
she continued until my mouth fell open and I started to scream;
You shouldn't have told me. I'm not old enough yet.

Jackie Kay

NOAH

They gathered around and told him not to do it,
They formed a committee and tried to take control,
They cancelled his building permit and they stole
His plans. I sometimes wonder he got through it.
He told them wrath was coming, they would rue it,
He betted them to believe the tides would roll,
He offered them passage to his destined goal,
A new world. They were finished and he knew it.
All to no end.

And then the rain began.
A spatter at first that barely wet the soil,
Then showers, quick rivulets lacing the town,
Then deluge universal. The old man
Arthritic from his years of scorn and toil
Leaned from the admiral's walk and watched them drown.

Roy Daniells

POOR BEASTS!

The horse and mule live 30 years
And nothing know of wines and beers.
The goat and sheep at 20 die
And never taste of Scotch or Rye.
The cow drinks water by the ton
And at 18 is mostly done.
The dog at 15 cashes in
Without the aid of rum and gin.
The cat in milk and water soaks
And then in 12 short years it croaks.
The modest, sober, bone-dry hen
Lays eggs for nogs, then dies at 10.
All animals are strictly dry:
They sinless live and swiftly die;
But sinful, ginful, rum-soaked men
Survive for three score years and ten.
And some of them, a very few,
Stay pickled till they're 92.

Anonymous

A CHILD'S PET

When I sailed out of Baltimore
    With twice a thousand head of sheep,
They would not eat, they would not drink,
    But bleated o'er the deep.

Inside the pens we crawled each day,
    To sort the living from the dead;
And when we reached the Mersey's mouth,
    Had lost five hundred head.

Yet every night and day one sheep,
    That had no fear of man or sea,
Stuck through the bars its pleading face,
    And it was stroked by me.

And to the sheep-men standing near,
    'You see,' I said, 'this one tame sheep;
It seems a child has lost her pet,
    And cried herself to sleep.'

So every time we passed it by,
    Sailing to England's slaughter-house,
Eight ragged sheep-men - tramps and thieves -
    Would stroke that sheep's black nose.

W.H. Davies

A FELLOW MORTAL

I found a fox, caught by the leg
In a toothed gin, torn from its peg,
And dragged, God knows how far, in pain.

Such torment could not plead in vain,
He looked at me, I looked at him,
With iron jaw-teeth in his limb.

'Come, little son,' I said, 'Let be …
Don't bite me, while I set you free.'

But much I feared that in the pang
Of helping, I should feel a fang
In hand or face …

                  but must is must …
And he had given me his trust.

So down I knelt there in the mud
And loosed those jaws all mud and blood.
And he, exhausted, crept, set free,
Into the shade, away from me;

The leg not broken …

                Then, beyond,
That gin went plonk into the pond.

John Masefield

HEDGEHOG

Suddenly, a dark amorphous
Shape in the middle of the road
Drowned in the splashed circle of the
Lamps. I stop the car and get out.

Some of his prickles look dry, their
Points bent or broken. Tiny dark
Lice glitter at their roots. A globe
Of weight and some warmth; pressed, a ball

Of agony balanced on nails
In my palms. I turn him over.
A dark eye flickers in the lights,
Then lids out. Put him in the boot.

I drive home. Placed on the dew-soaked grass,
He lies still as a coprolite.
Twenty-five minutes of silence.
And stillness and muteness and cold.
Then go in for an overcoat.

But when I come back he has gone
Off into the fragrant hedges of
Hawthorn and fallen leaves. I search
The garden with a torch. Nothing.

And I would give the hand that holds
This pen to know what fierce blaze of
Purpose took him off into the
Inscrutable, earthy dark.

Roy Holland

SQUIRRELS

Tails like dandelion clocks
They blow away, these
Light-weight bucking broncos
With a plume behind.

For sheer surprise
No well-aimed burdock
Sticks more nimbly to your overcoat
Than these to tree bark,

Nor with such aplomb
Can any comparable creature
Lead a dance more deftly
Through the branches.

Down to earth again, they
Hold their tums in, little aldermen,
Or sit on tree stumps
Like old ladies knitting socks.

John Mole

PIGLET

The cardboard box tremored,
With nervous vibrations,
The blanket was a mountain,
Which he could not climb.
His umbilical cord hung down,
Like a grey worm.
He stuck his snout in the corner of cardboard,
Searching for his mother.
He was four hours old
And lucky to be alive.
As they tried feeding him through a rubber glove fake udder
He squeaked as if someone had trodden on a toy dog bone
And milk squirted sideways drenching his body hairs,
Dripping like dabs of watery white paint
On his shining body, not used to the lights.
As his mouth opened,
High pitched snuffles bellowed out.
The scratches on his back looked like open veins.
They were from fighting his brothers and sisters,
In a scrabble for their mother's milk.
The over-sized cloth ears
Hid his squirming eyes.
Bits of dry grass stuck to his shivering body,
The tail sticking out like a ringlet of permed hair.
Calmly, I stroked his pinkish-white body.
And as I ran my fingers up and down his back,
Small dimple ripples subsided.
Then, as she picked him up,
He scrumpled up his keyhole snout.
And made such a piercing noise for such a tiny creature.
He was back to his rightful owner.

Tessa Hart (Aged 12)

TRAVELLING THROUGH THE DARK

Travelling through the dark I found a deer
dead on the edge of the Wilson River road.
It is usually best to roll them into the canyon:
that road is narrow; to swerve might make more dead.

By glow of the tail-light I stumbled back of the car
and stood by the heap, a doe, a recent killing;
she had stiffened already, almost cold.
I dragged her off; she was large in the belly.

My fingers touching her side brought me the reason -
her side was warm; her fawn lay there waiting,
alive, still, never to be born.
Beside that mountain road I hesitated.

The car aimed ahead its lowered parking lights;
under the hood purred the steady engine.
I stood in the glare of the warm exhaust turning red;
around our group I could hear the wilderness listen.

I thought hard for us all - my only swerving -
then pushed her over the edge into the river.

William Stafford

THE GIRAFFE

Long-necked gentle creature
Why are your soft brown eyes so sad?
Do your winged ears
Sense the changing times?

Long-necked gentle creature
Will your neck go on growing forever?
Can we trace the roads of Africa
On your smooth brown skin?

Long-necked gentle creature
Your symmetry lies upon you
Like a jigsaw puzzle
Can we ever find the missing piece?

Long-necked gentle creature
With your swift and graceful run
Can you escape from the future
And remain untouched by man?

Charlotte Last (Aged 11)

AN ELEPHANT REMEMBERS

I was Rajah
Emperor of all elephants,
On the feasts of Dasera and Diwali
I was clothed like a king
in sumptuous trappings
Of gold and silver brocade.
My howdah was covered with silk,
Blue as the royal peacock,
Beautiful girls rode on my back,
Their black hair fragrant
with frangipani blossoms,
Their laughter bright as temple bells.
How majestically I swayed
Through streets seething with people,
The scent of sandalwood and jasmine,
Cardamom and cumin,
The riot of morning glory flowers
And the hot dust.
I am old now
And stiff in my bones,
But I can still feel
The soft touch of a sari,
Turn my head to the chime
Of bell and gong.

Theresa Heine

ZEBRA

People have lost interest in the zebra
since the coming of colour television.

At the Serengeti waterhole
he dips his ancient heraldic head,
fills his round belly.

On the dry dust of the plain
he casts a blue shadow.
His heavy eyes watch the acacia trees
for the least sign of movement.
He shakes his mane,
the dark plume of a Roman centurion.

At home we take the zebra for granted,
let him carry us across the road
outside the supermarket.

Gilroy Fisher

THE THING ABOUT AARDVARKS

If you put them in a football team
they wouldn't score a goal
If you took them to a golf course
they'd never find the hole
If they're boxing with a squirrel
they'll come back badly beaten
They cannot win Monopoly
even if they're cheating
If someone let a stink-bomb off
they'd be the last to smell it
If you ask them to write down their name
they'll ask you how to spell it.

And even in the 'egg & spoon'
they're bringing up the rear
They never break the finishing tape
to hear a thunderous cheer
And yet there is a place
where they are sure of victory
For the aardvark always comes first
in the English dictionary.

Lindsay MacRae

MONSTER ALPHABET

A small dragon, phoenix, centaur,
Bunyip, wyvern, minotaur,
Chinchayak and wendigo
Dromedaraffe, hipporhinostricow,
Extinct monsters, nosey dong,
Frankenstein, pandemonium,
Gruesome, gofongo round the house,
Hidebehind and tigeroceros,
Impish creatures, bongaloo,
Jam fish, toaster, bogus-boo,
Kraken, dinkey, jabberwock,
Loch ness monster, horny-goloch,
Marrog, moonbird, manatee,
Oliphaunt, pobble with no toes,
P'eng, malfeasance, aimless doze,
Quangle wangle with his hat,
Roc, baboopine and bisky bat,
Serpent, swank and snitterjipe,
Triantiwontigongolope,
Ugstabuggle, unicorn,
Visitors in beastly form,
White monsters, red and blue,
Xisting if you wish them to,
Yet one more completes our zoo,
Zobo bird - so

        who are you?

Robert Fisher

THE KRAKEN

Below the thunders of the upper deep;
Far far beneath in the abysmal sea,
His ancient, dreamless, uninvaded sleep
The Kraken sleepeth: faintest sunlights flee
About his shadowy sides: above him swell
Huge sponges of millennial growth and height;
And far away into the sickly light
From many a wondrous grot and secret cell
Unnumber'd and enormous polypi
Winnow with giant fins the slumbering green.
There hath he lain for ages and will lie
Battening upon huge seaworms in his sleep,
Until the latter fire shall heat the deep;
Then once by men and angels to be seen,
In roaring he shall rise and on the surface die.

Alfred, Lord Tennyson

THE ROC

Scattered like flotsam on the erupting sea
  When the ship cracked, Sinbad and his sailors
    Gasped for air, clung to the planks and oars,
Then struggled madly for the beach. Some three
Who managed to escape the crags were thrown
  On yellow sand, and fell asleep at once,
    Soaked through but too exhausted to take shelter,
And slept like dead men till next day at noon.

On waking, someone noticed a black cloud
  Descending over them, like a huge raven
    With curved bill, wings, extended talons,
And voice of thunder, distant but quite loud.
Sinbad grew pale, trembled and shouted, "Quick,
  Find shelter somewhere; this is the great Roc,
    The bird of prey with wingspan of a mile!
Run to the cave; don't stop to have a look!"

They reached the grotto just in time, - the sky
  Had grown pitch-black, the wingbeats were a gale;
    But, safe in hiding, Sinbad laughed: "A miracle!
It's not the Roc that's huge, but you and I,
My sailors, who are small, and growing smaller;
  Soon we'll be microscopic, and that crow -
    As harmless as a lion to a gnat -
Won't even notice when we choose to go."

Edward Lowbury

GREEDY DOG

This dog will eat anything.

Apple cores and bacon fat,
Milk you poured out for the cat.
He likes the string that ties the roast
And relishes hot buttered toast.
Hide your chocolates! He's a thief,
He'll even eat your handkerchief.
And if you don't like sudden shocks,
Carefully conceal your socks.
Leave some soup without a lid,
And you'll wish you never did.
When you think he must be full,
You find him gobbling bits of wool,
Orange peel or paper bags,
Dusters and old cleaning rags.
This dog will eat anything,
Except for mushrooms and cucumber.

Now what is wrong with those, I wonder?

James Hurley

FAMILY HOLIDAY

Eight months ago, on Christmas Day,
he was a present for the twins,
a toy to join in all their play.

They left by car, but how long since
he cannot tell, nor when they'll come
(if ever) back, to make amends.

The house is blind and deaf and dumb,
the curtains drawn, the windows shut,
the doors sealed tighter than a tomb.

Even the little garden hut
is padlocked. He barks feebly at
each slowing car or passing foot.

Stretched on the WELCOME on the mat
in the front porch, he feels the hunger
gnawing inside him like a rat.

Suffers, endures, but knows no anger.

Raymond Wilson

STORIES

Circling by the fire,
My dog, my rough champion
Coaxes winter out of her fur.
She hears old stories
Leaping in the flames:
The hissing names of cats,
Neighbors' dogs snapping
Like these gone logs,
The cracking of ice …
Once, romping through the park,
We dared the creaking pond.
It took the dare and half
Of me into the dark below.
She never let go.

We watch orange tongues
Wagging in the fire
Hush to blue whispers.
Her tail buffs my shoe.
She has one winter left.

Maybe two.

J Patrick Lewis

MILKING SONG

Like a sandstone sculpture, the ginger cat
Sits on his tipsy plinth of fence,
Snug in the arc of his tidy tail
And feigning a fine indifference
To morning's leisured blossoming,
The hills' slow stirring to unfold
The hour's intrinsic loveliness,
The curve of sky, the spill of gold.

Spun galaxies of mislaid stars,
The yellow thornbills prank the air,
Conspiring to confuse the sun;
And down the hill my lady-mare,
A wagtail at her wither, comes;
And magpies fill the sky with song
And hang the trees with leafy notes
For flocks of winds to flute among.

The soft froth lips the bucket's rim;
The red cow roughs her tongue around
The empty feed-bin's edge … The cat,
Suddenly vital at the sound,
Leaps in a golden arc from fence
To ground and then, with flanks grown thin
And eyes gone green, he laps at last
His nectar from a rusty tin.

Anne Bell

COOL CAT

Well I'm a cat with nine
And I'm in my prime
I'm a Casanova Cat
And I'm feline fine
I'm strolling down the street
In my white slipper feet
Yeh, all the little lady cats
Are looking for a treat
because I got style
I got a naughty smile
I'm gonna cross this street
In just a little while
      to be with you
      to be with you
      to be with you
      to be with
You got grace
You got a lickable face
I'm gonna love ya and leave ya
And you'll never find a trace
Because I'm on my own
I like to be alone
I'm just a swingin', strollin',
Rollin' stone
But it's your lucky day
I'm gonna pass your way
I can spare a little lovin'
If you wanna stop and
      play with me
      play with me
      play with me
      play with
Me oh my
I got a twinkling eye
I'm gonna cross this street

So don't you be too shy
But what's this I see
Comin' straight at me
It's a crazy car driver
Tryin' to make me flee
So I look up slow
Just to let the man know
That I don't go any faster
Than I really wanna go.

****

Well I'm a cat with eight
I guess he couldn't wait
But I'm lookin' good
And I'm feline great!

Mike Jubb

THE FLY

Little Fly,
Thy summer's play
My thoughtless hand
Has brushed away.

Am not I
A fly like thee?
Or art not thou
A man like me?

For I dance,
And drink, and sing,
Till some blind hand
Shall brush my wing.

If thought is life
And strength and breath,
And the want
Of thought is death;

Then am I
A happy fly,
If I live
Or if I die.

William Blake

ROOKS LOVE EXCITEMENT

Rooks love excitement. When I walked in under the rookery
A gale churned the silvery, muscular boughs of the beeches, and the
    wet leaves streamed -
It was like a big sea heaving through wreckage -

And the whole crew of rooks lifted off with a shout and floated clear.
I could see the oiled lights in (their waterproofs)
As the blue spilled them this way and that, and their cries stormed.

Were they shouting at me? What did they fear?
It sounded
More like a packed football stadium, at the shock of a longed-for
    goal -

A sudden upfling of everything, a surfing cheer.

Ted Hughes

BLACKBIRD

My wife saw it first -
I was reading the evening paper.
Come and look, she said.

It was trying to drink
Where water had formed on a drain-cover.
It was shabby with dying.
It did not move until I was very close -
Then hopped off, heavily,
Disturbing dead leaves.

We left water, crumbs.
It did not touch them
But waited among the leaves,
Silently.

This morning was beautiful:
Sunlight, other birds
Singing.

It was outside the door.
I picked it up
And it was like holding feathered air.
I wrapped what was left
Incongruously
In green sycamore leaves
And buried it near the tree,
Inches down.

This evening
I find it difficult to concentrate
On the paper, the news
Of another cosmonaut.

Christopher Leach

HERON

Solitary in ruffled water,
Bill and legs mirrored yellow upon the lapping river,
The old heron waits
Deep to the knees
Above the bough-entangled weir
Postured to a question-mark.
The last evening noises meet the oncoming stars
As gorgon-wise he bends his crested head
Whiter than marble or tufted thistledown
Over the fringing rushes.
And on an island anchored in the darkening stream
His brood of fledglings pierce
The air with eager cries
Where hollow ruins merge themselves with night,
And every outline, every tree is blurred.
His thoughts and jewelled eyes are not on these
But centred on each growing ring that now and then
Fingers the ripples with tracery.
There in a moving world of peopled weed,
Half light, half sound,
Fish scurry from hole to hole,
Blind to the sword that points its threatening stretch
Above their flashing voyagings.
And then,
As shriller come the pipings
From the careless architecture of the heronry,
He dagger-lunges the surfaces,
And rises clumsily over the shallows and fields
Bearing aloft upon dripping spear
A doomed and gaping trout,
And higher still he mounts on rounded wing
Spanning the moonlit regions in undivided majesty.

Leonard Clark

THE SCULPTOR

He stares
At the motionless block.
Within it, he sees a creature
Entombed in the darkness,
Reluctant to leave.
He clasps the chisel;
He studies the stone prison;
The sharp instrument
Pierces the surface.
He strikes again;
A segment breaks away.
With delicate strokes
He chips
At the shell case.
A curved beak
Is set free;
Two hooded eyes
Stare at their creator.
The eagle is hatching.

Kim Garrard (Aged 15)

SONG OF THE BATTERY HEN

We can't grumble about accommodation:
we have a new concrete floor that's
always dry, four walls that are
painted white, and sheet-iron roof
the rain drums on. A fan blows warm air
beneath our feet to disperse the smell
of chicken-shit and, on dull days,
fluorescent lighting sees us.

You can tell me: if you come by
the North door, I am in the twelfth pen
on the left-hand side of the third row
from the floor; and in that pen
I am usually the middle one of three.
But, even without directions, you'd
discover me. I have the same orange-
red comb, yellow beak and auburn
feathers, but as the door opens and you
hear above the electric fan a kind of
one-word wail, I am the one
who sounds loudest in my head.

Listen. Outside this house there's an
orchard with small moss-green apple
trees; beyond that, two fields of
cabbages; then, on the far side of
the road, a broiler house. Listen:
one cockerel grows out of there, as
tall and proud as the first hour of sun.
Sometimes I stop calling with the others
to listen, and wonder if he hears me.

The next time you come here, look for me.
Notice the way I sound inside my head.
God made us all quite differently,
and blessed us with this expensive home.

Edwin Brock

PENGUINS

Penguins dress in curious clothes,
are at home among the bleakest snows.
They throng like well-dined
portly gentlemen with toes
turned in, lined
up for taxis buttoning
black overcoats,
white scarves dangling
from their throats.

Every penguin expects his
neighbour to be polite.
They don't do things by half.
If anyone transgresses,
they fight
or start wrangling,
their voices loud and hoarse,
their penguin sentences
just a trifle coarse.

Puppet legs, wooden arms,
they niddy-noddy
to the tempestuous sea,
but when they enter,
diving,
they change suddenly
into hunting shapes swifter
than those that haunt my dreams,
eerily, silently,
embodying terror
and a startling beauty.

Albert Rowe

MY SISTER JANE

And I say nothing - no, not a word
About our Jane. Haven't you heard?
She's a bird, a bird, a bird, a bird.
Oh it never would do to let folks know
My sister's nothing but a great big crow.

Each day (we daren't send her to school)
She pulls on stockings of thick blue wool
To make her pin crow legs look right,
Then fits a wig of curls on tight,
And dark spectacles - a huge pair
To cover her very crowy stare.
Oh it never would do to let folks know
My sister's nothing but a great big crow.

When visitors come she sits upright
(With her wings and her tail tucked out of sight).
They think her queer but extremely polite.
Then when the visitors have gone
She whips out her wings and with her wig on
Whirls through the house at the height of your head -
Duck, duck, or she'll knock you dead.
Oh it never would do to let folks know
My sister's nothing but a great big crow.

At meals whatever she sees she'll stab it -
Because she's a crow and that's a crow habit.
My mother says 'Jane! Your manners! Please!'
Then she'll sit quietly on the cheese,
Or play the piano nicely by dancing on the keys -
Oh it never would do to let folks know
My sister's nothing but a great big crow.

Ted Hughes

NEW BABY

My baby brother makes so much noise
that the Rottweiler next door
phoned up to complain.

My baby brother makes so much noise
that all the big green frogs
came out the drains.

My baby brother makes so much noise
that the rats and the mice
wore headphones.

My baby brother makes so much noise
that I can't ask my mum a question,
so much noise that sometimes

I think of sitting the cat on top of him
in his pretty little cot with all his teddies.
But even the cat is terrified of his cries.

So I have devised a plan. A soundproof room.
A telephone to talk to my mum.
A small lift to receive food and toys.

Thing is, it will cost a fortune.
The other thing is, the frogs have gone.
It's not bad now. Not that I like him or anything.

Jackie Kay

THE TRICK

One night, when I couldn't sleep,
My dad said
*Think of the tomatoes in the
greenhouse*

And I did.
It wasn't the same as counting sheep
Or anything like that.

It was just not being in my room
forever
On a hot bed
Restless, turning and turning,

But out there, with the patient gaze of
moonlight
Blessing each ripe skin
And our old zinc watering-can with its
sprinkler,

Shining through a clear glass pane
Which slowly clouded over into
Drowsy, comfortable darkness

Till I woke and came downstairs to
breakfast
Saying *Thank you, Dad,
I thought of them. It did the trick.*

John Mole

SUNDAY FATHERS

I used to notice them,
one of the Sunday sights:
fathers visiting their children
and walking them in parks
or sitting over milk-shakes
making careful conversation.

I saw a pair on Sunday
looking in a shop window,
I thought, but the boy's eyes
were curtained with tears
and the father's arms were shut
out by more than the week.

Now I try not to see them:
such a shadow on the sun's day

Michael Harrison

HIGH NOON AT BARKING ODEON

Auntie Doris and my mum
are fighting in the cinema queue.
It's a strange adult conflict
this battle of wills,
for whoever wins the contest
gets to pay the bill.

'I insist on paying,' says Doris
'It's my treat!' shrieks mum,
shoving the sweaty £20 note back at her.
'Please let me pay,' begs Doris,
scrunching up the note and shoving it
in mum's pocket.
'No you keep your money, Doris,' says mum firmly,
as she prises Doris's shirt open and flicks it down the front.
'There now, that's settled!'

Doris jiggles around, vibrating madly,
then untucks her shirt.
The money falls on to the floor.

All the queue is staring
at mum glaring
at Doris glaring
at mum.
You could hear a pin drop
but you can't hear any swearing
and in a fit of daring
I pick up the offending (and now forgotten)
£20 of sterling
and pocket it.

Then mum and Doris burst out laughing
'What a pair we are!' they chorus
as mum gets out her purse
to pay for the tickets.

I feel like a diplomat
on a peace mission
except that I get a hot-dog
in the intermission.
So much excitement
and the film hasn't even begun.
I'm 20 quid richer
and Doris is still speaking to mum.

Lindsay MacRae

THE PASSING OF THE TELEGRAM

I wanted to alert my phoneless daughter -
a student, on a grant -
that a later train than first advised
would contain an aged aunt.
The man at British Telecom was useless,
I put the phone down with a slam,
he said the only thing to do
was to send a gorillagram.

I had to send some furry ape
to Newcastle upon Tyne
to read the following message:
Aunt Win arriving sixteen forty-nine.

Charlotte Mitchell

JUST LIKE A MAN

He sat at the dinner table
    With a discontented frown,
The potatoes and steak were underdone
    And the bread was baked too brown;
The pie was too sour and the pudding too sweet,
    And the roast was much too fat;
The soup so greasy, too, and salt,
    'Twas hardly fit for the cat.

'I wish you could eat the bread and pie
    I've seen my mother make,
They are something like, and 'twould do you good
    Just to look at a loaf of her cake.'
Said the smiling wife, 'I'll improve with age -
    Just now I'm a beginner;
But your mother has come to visit us,
    And to-day she cooked the dinner.'

Anonymous

AUNT SUE'S STORIES

Aunt Sue has a head full of stories.
Aunt Sue has a whole heart full of stories.
Summer nights on the front porch
Aunt Sue cuddles a brown-faced child to her
bosom
And tells him stories.

Black slaves
Working in the hot sun,
And black slaves
Walking in the dewy night,
And black slaves singing sorrow songs on the
banks of a mighty river
Mingle themselves softly
In the flow of old Aunt Sue's voice,
Mingle themselves softly
In the dark shadows that cross and recross
Aunty Sue's stories.

And the dark-faced child, listening,
Knows that Aunt Sue never got her stories
Out of any book at all,
But that they came
Right out of her own life.

The dark-faced child is quiet
    Of a summer night
    Listening to Aunt Sue's stories.

Langston Hughes

JEOPARDY

'You know his job's in Jeopardy,'
I heard them say when I was small.
Where was it? I imagined it
all jungly and leopardy
with butterflies like aeroplanes
above a waterfall
which leapt with rainbows, tumbling
to swell a boulder-studded stream.
I roared with it, I raced with it,
we set the canyons rumbling.
He lost his job, and Jeopardy
became a childhood dream.

Sue Cowling

WASHDAY BATTLES

On washday in the good old bad old days
Before the launderette, machine and drier,
My mother used to use her own bare hands,
A posher, mangle, line, a wooden horse and fire.

At dawn she blew small coals into a blaze
Under well-water in a brim-full copper.
Soon as the water seethed and steamed into a haze
The clothes were seized. They plunged, and came a cropper.

Submerged, they scaled, lunged and tossed,
Squelched by fire-water through and through,
Until she gripped her soggy wooden stick
And levered them, steaming, out, all black and blue,

Carried them soggy and limply dripping,
Chucked them onto the washboard-tub,
Where she set to, and thumped and slapped
And poshed and punched them, rub-a-dub.

Then she grabbed each punch-drunk one in turn
Wrung its neck, squeezed all its juice outright.
Corkscrewed and throttled, flat out it lay, quite dead,
And then she set to again, and beat it white.

Straightaway she fed it to the lion-roaring mangle,
Into tight-rolling rubber lips, which sucked it in
Then slurped it out again, pancaked
To a wafer, breathless, depressed, and thin.

And then she flung them over her arm,
Hauled them out to the windy backyard plot,
Shook them out, cracked them like a whip,
Then strung them up and hanged the lot.

Soon as the wind possessed those wretched shapes,
Their arms would wildly wave, their legs kick free,
The skirts would billow out, voluminous,
And all the washing blew out, flew out, on the spree.

Mimicking Nelson's flags (England expects ...)
They semaphored 'A Terrible To-do!'
'Clothes Saved From Drowning.' 'All Hands Saved!'
'Housewife Fails Again to Drown This Gallant Crew!'

Geoffrey Summerfield

THE FAMILY BOOK

My father unlocks the family book
where the captured Victorians sit
tight-lipped, keeping their own closed counsel.
I find them caught at christenings
as the 'greats' collect with the 'latest'
and another name is tied to the family line;
or posed (but not poised) in studios,
the fathers and sons from their Sunday slumbers,
suited and sober and seemingly shy
as if their souls could be stolen away
for the price of a print on paper.

I watch my father separate the 'great greats'
from the 'great', the proud patriarchs,
the weddings and unsmiling aunts,
the fishermen released from their nets,
the light-keeper and his shiny wife.
I flick back the pages and try to find
my fingerprints in their faces.

Brian Moses

DAD CAN'T DANCE

A couple of pints of lager
and he's quite red in the face
he thinks he is the business
but he just looks out of place.
He waves his arms around a bit
and wriggles his behind
a more embarrassing spectacle
would be difficult to find.

The Rolling Stones were Number 1
when he last took to the floor
I tell him that the Twist
just isn't trendy any more
(a bit of information
which he chooses to ignore).

But now he's got into the rhythm
the music is loud
he's causing a stir
and he's drawing a crowd.
My friends say: 'Don't worry
he isn't that bad!'
It's all right for them
he isn't their dad.

He moves like an emu
with three left feet
as a total twerp
he'd be hard to beat
I wish he'd stayed at home tonight
(or at least stayed in his seat).
And if he doesn't take his jacket off
he's going to overheat.

Now he's twitching like a zombie
who's gone into a trance.
He's not too bad at changing plugs
but we shouldn't let him dance!

Lindsay MacRae

RICHARD

Shouting, screaming, listening, dreaming,
Twiddling, flapping, laughing, clapping,
Always watching, never joining in.
Locked in your world so far away,
The boy in the playground who cannot play.
With no social grace you like to grimace
And make rude noises at passers-by.
You look like an angel with your beautiful face
Which God gave you as your saving grace.
Is your world a dream or is it a nightmare?
If only there was a part we could share.
You've shown us affection in your own way.
You've made us laugh and pushed us away.
People stare because they don't know
How hard it is for you to show
Your feelings, except with tears of frustration
Because you lack communication.
They say you're non-verbal, I call you 'non-wordal',
You're noisy, disruptive, you're happy, you're different.
Richard my brother, I love you a lot.
Trapped in your world that seems so simplistic,
It is a tragedy that you're autistic.

Caroline Allen   (Aged 11)

MUM DAD AND ME

My parents grew among palmtrees,
in sunshine strong and clear.
I grow in weather that's pale,
misty, watery or plain cold,
around back streets of London.

Dad swam in warm sea, at my age.
I swim in a roofed pool,
Mum - she still doesn't swim.

Mum went to an open village market
at my age. I go to a covered
arcade one with her now.
Dad works most Saturdays.

At my age Dad played
cricket with friends.
Mum helped her mum, or talked
shouting halfway up a hill.
Now I read or talk on the phone.

With her friends Mum's mum washed
clothes on a river-stone. Now
washing-machine washes our clothes.
We save time to eat to TV,
never speaking.

My dad longed for a freedom in Jamaica.
I want a greater freedom.
Mum prays for us, always.

Mum goes to church
some evenings and Sundays.
I go to the library.
Dad goes for his darts at the local

Mum walked everywhere, at my age.
Dad rode a donkey.
Now I take a bus
or catch the underground train.

_____

James Berry

SAUCE

Aunt Ruth came from England
and guess all that we got -
a jar of English mustard
which she said was very hot.

'That yellow thing no pepper!'
remarked my aunty Dot.
'England famous for it strawberry
but for pepper it is not!'

Before we could prevent her
Aunt D dip in she big spoon.
It hot! It hot! So till
it nearly send her to the moon.

Now aunty Dot eats quietly
she scarcely speaks a word
she no touch the jar of mustard
since it deaden she taste-bud.

_____

Pauline Stewart

THE VISITORS

'Twenty-seven lamps is what it takes,' he said,
setting his little candles on the stairs,
'to light the way and welcome back the dead.'
I helped him light their little welcome flares

because he's my best mate. His Dad and Mum
were Buddhists and I know his Obon feast
means food set out for visitors to come
seeking Nirvana which, he says, is peace.

'At Obon we invite them to return
and visit us.' He paused with eyes alight -
like mine, I guess, on Christmas Eve, when wine
is left for Santa Claus. 'They'll come tonight.'

I know his grandad and his mother drowned,
with nearly everybody from their junk,
under the China Seas when bandits rammed
their overcrowded boat. He would have sunk

but for his dad and sister who took turns
to hold him up. I reckon one who's
rescued from a hell like that soon learns
what welcome lights we can't afford to lose.

'We'll burn the paper lantern now,' he said.
'Grandad used to make them out of lotus
leaves, but this will have to do instead.'
I pray and hope it helps them reach us

in these flats. I watch his eyes go still and wide
with peaceful welcome. In the flickering glare
his face is like a beacon lit to guide
the old man and his daughter up the stair.

Barrie Wade

ABIGAIL

Abigail knew when she was born
Among the roses, she was a thorn.
Her quiet mother had lovely looks.
Her quiet father wrote quiet books.
Her quiet brothers, correct though pale,
Weren't really prepared for Abigail
Who entered the house with howls and tears
While both of her brothers blocked their ears
And both of her parents, talking low,
Said, 'Why is Abigail screaming so?'

Abigail kept on getting worse.
As soon as she teethed she bit her nurse,
At three, she acted distinctly cool
Toward people and things at nursery school.
'I'm sick of cutting out dolls,' she said,
And cut a hole in her dress, instead.
Her mother murmured, 'She's bold for three.'
Her father answered, 'I quite agree.'
Her brothers mumbled, 'We hate to fuss,
But when will Abigail be like us?'

Abigail, going through her teens,
Liked overalls and pets and machines.
In college, hating most of its features,
She told off all of her friends and teachers.
Her brothers, graduating from Yale,
Said: 'Really, you're hopeless, Abigail.'
And while her mother said, 'Fix your looks,'
Her father added, 'Or else write books.'
And Abigail asked, 'Is that a dare?'
And wrote a book that would curl your hair.

Kay Starbird

MANCO THE PERUVIAN CHIEF

i looked down at my stomach
the way one does
in the bath
and noticed that i was scarlet
from head to toe
good gracious
i gasped
now i am a redskin
i am hiawatha
pocahontas
sitting bull
and manco the peruvian chief
i live in a forest of tall spruce
and sleep at night
in a wigwam full of strange odours
and wood smoke
hist
i hear pale faces in the lounge
powwowing with my squaw
curse the whites
uttering fierce battle cries
i charged downstairs
and whooped into the meeting house
indian brave no likum pale face
i shouted defiantly
ho
ho
ho
mother hastily threw a rug around me
and said
excuse me ladies
i think julian has measles

for two weeks i never left my bed
and was waited on
hand
and foot

Redmond Phillips

SUGARFIELDS

treetalk and windsong
are the language of my mother
her music does not leave me.

Let me taste again the cane
the syrup of the earth
sugarfields were once my home.

I would lie down in the fields
and never get up again
(treetalk and windsong
are the language of my mother
sugarfields are my home)

the leaves go on whispering secrets
as the wind blows a tune in the grass
my mother's voice is in the fields
this music cannot leave me.

Barbara Mahone

BEARHUGS

Whenever my sons call round we hug each other.
Bearhugs. Both bigger than me and stronger
They lift me off my feet, crushing the life out of me.

They smell of oil paint and aftershave, of beer
Sometimes and tobacco, and of women
Whose memory they seem reluctant to wash away.

They haven't lived with me for years,
Since they were tiny, and so each visit
Is an assessment, a reassurance of love unspoken.

I look for some resemblance to my family.
Seize on an expression, a lifted eyebrow,
A tilt of the head, but cannot see myself.

Though like each other, they are not like me.
But I can see in them something of my father.
Uncles, home on leave during the war.

At three or four, I loved those straightbacked men
Towering above me, smiling and confident.
The whole world before them. Or so it seemed.

I look at my boys, slouched in armchairs
They have outgrown. See Tom in army uniform
And Finn in air force blue. Time is up.

Bearhugs. They lift me off my feet
And fifty years fall away. One son
After another, crushing the life into me.

Roger McGough

REFUGEE

He can't speak a word of English
But the picture he paints needs no words

In it he puts:

guns
bright orange explosions
a house with no roof
children with no shoes
and his mother and father
lying still, as though asleep.
At the bottom he puts himself, tiny and dark,
with a puddle of blue tears at his feet.
Somehow the fat yellow sun at the top of the page
has a smile on its face.

Lindsay MacRae

CALLING THE ROLL

"Corporal Green!" the orderly cried;
   "Here!" was the answer, loud and clear,
From the lips of a soldier standing near;
And "here!" was the word the next replied;
"Cyrus Drew!" and a silence fell;
   This time, no answer followed the call;
   Only his rear-man saw him fall,
Killed or wounded, he could not tell.

There they stood in the failing light,
   These man of battle, with grave, dark looks,
   As plain to be read as open books,
While slowly gathered the shades of night;
The fern on the slope was splashed with blood,
   And down in the corn, where the poppies grew,
   Were redder stains than the poppies knew;
And crimson-dyed was the river's flood.

For the foe had crossed from the other side,
   That day, in the face of a murderous fire
That swept them down in its terrible ire;
And their life-blood went to color the tide.
"Herbert Cline!" At the call there came
   Two stalwart soldiers into the line,
   Bearing between them Herbert Cline,
Wounded and bleeding, to answer his name.

"Ezra Kerr!" and a voice said "here!"
   "Hiram Kerr!" but no man replied:
   They were brothers, these two; the sad wind sighed,
And a shudder crept through the corn-field near.
"Ephraim Deane!" - then a soldier spoke:
   "Deane carried our regiment's colors," he said,
   "When our ensign was shot; I left him dead,
Just after the enemy wavered and broke.

"Close to the roadside his body lies:
   I paused a moment, and gave him to drink;
   He murmured his mother's name, I think;
And death came with it and closed his eyes."
'Twas a victory - yes; but it cost us dear;
   For that company's roll, when called at night,
   Of a hundred men who went into the fight,
Numbered but twenty that answered "here!"

Nathaniel Graham Shepherd

FUTILITY

Move him into the sun -
Gently its touch awoke him once,
At home, whispering of fields unsown.
Always it woke him, even in France,
Until this morning and this snow.
If anything might rouse him now
The kind old sun will know.

Think how it wakes the seeds, -
Woke, once, the clays of a cold star.
Are limbs, so dear-achieved, are sides,
Full-nerved - still warm - too hard to stir?
Was it for this the clay grew tall?
O what made fatuous sunbeams toil
To break earth's sleep at all?

Wilfred Owen

HIROSHIMA

Noon, and hazy heat;
A single silver sliver and a dull drone;
The gloved finger poised, pressed:
A second's silence, and
Oblivion.

Anonymous

FAMILY FEELING

My Uncle Alfred had the terrible temper.
Wrapped himself up in its invisible cloak.
When the mood was on his children crept from the kitchen.
It might have been mined. Not even the budgie spoke.

He was killed in the First World War in Mesopotamia.
His widow rejoiced, though she never wished him dead.
After three years a postcard arrived from Southampton.
'Coming home Tuesday. Alf,' was what it said.

His favourite flower he called the antimirrhinum.
Grew it instead of greens on the garden plot.
Didn't care much for children, though father of seven.
Owned in his lifetime nine dogs all called Spot.

At Carnival time he rode the milkman's pony,
Son of the Sheikh, a rifle across his knee.
Alf the joiner as Peary in cotton-wood snowstorms.
Secret in cocoa and feathers, an Indian Cree.

I recognized him once as the Shah of Persia.
My Auntie's front-room curtains gave him away.
'It's Uncle Alf!' I said, but his glance was granite.
'Mind your own business, nosey,' I heard him say.

I never knew just what it was that bugged him,
Or what kind of love a father's love could be.
One by one his children bailed out of the homestead.
'You were too young when yours died,' they explained to me.

Today, walking through St Cyprian's Church-yard
I saw where he lay in a box the dry colour of bone.
The grass was tamed and trimmed as if for a Sunday.
Seven antimirrhinums in a jar of stone.

Charles Causley

TERRORIST'S WIFE

A phone-call takes him
into the dark for weeks.
In the mornings, his absence
fills me with dread. I thin my eyes
to watch for cars that come to wait
down in the street. All day
I move from room to room. I polish
each spotless place
to a chill shining. Fear tracks me
like hunger. In the silence,
the walls grow water-thin.
The neighbours wear masks -
tight lips, veiled looks, such
fine tissues of knowing.
My mother doesn't visit. I drag
my shopping from the next town.

Once, putting his clean shirts away,
my dry hands touched a shape
that lay cold and hard. I wept then,
and walked for hours in the park.
I listened for his name in the news.
When I looked at our sleeping son
my sadness thickened.
His comings are like his goings -
a swift movement in the night.

At times, he can sit here for days
meticulously groomed; primed,
watching soccer games on TV,
our child playful on his lap.
But scratch the smooth surface
of his mood, and how
the breached defences spit their fire.

Now, when he holds me to him,
I know I taste murder
on his mouth. And in the darkness,
when he turns from me, I watch him
light a cigarette. In his palm
the lighter clicks and flames.
Balanced, incendiary.

_____
Angela Greene

THE DUG-OUT

Why do you lie with your legs ungainly huddled,
And one arm bent across your sullen cold
Exhausted face? It hurts my heart to watch you,
Deep-shadowed from the candle's guttering gold;
And you wonder why I shake you by the shoulder;
Drowsy, you mumble and sigh and turn your head ...
You are too young to fall asleep for ever;
And when you sleep you remind me of the dead.

_____
Siegfried Sassoon

DULCE ET DECORUM EST

Bent double, like old beggars under sacks,
Knock-kneed, coughing like hags, we cursed through
    sludge,
Till on the haunting flares we turned our backs
And towards our distant rest began to trudge.
Men marched asleep. Many had lost their boots
But limped on, blood-shod. All went lame; all blind;
Drunk with fatigue; deaf even to the hoots
Of tired, outstripped Five-Nines that dropped behind.

Gas! GAS! Quick, boys! - An ecstasy of fumbling,
Fitting the clumsy helmets just in time;
But someone still was yelling out and stumbling,
And flound'ring like a man in fire or lime ...
Dim, through the misty panes and thick green light
As under a green sea, I saw him drowning.

In all my dreams, before my helpless sight,
He plunges at me, guttering, choking, drowning.

If in some smothering dreams you too could pace
Behind the wagon that we flung him in,
And watch the white eyes writhing in his face,
His hanging face, like a devil's sick of sin;
If you could hear, at every jolt, the blood
Come gargling from the froth-corrupted lungs,
Obscene as cancer, bitter as the cud
Of vile, incurable sores on innocent tongues, -
My friend, you would not tell with such high zest
To children ardent for some desperate glory,
The old Lie: Dulce et decorum est
Pro patria mori.

Wilfred Owen

NO RETURN

Death Camps, fifty years on

Your candles flicker on the railway track
that led to hell, the camps of hair and bone.
We are their ghosts, O do not call us back.

They tied the human spirit in a sack
of ash and smoke, these little flames atone:
your candles flicker on the railway track.

They had their killing place, a shower, a shack.
Our people stood together and alone.
We are their ghosts, O do not call us back.

For who can free tormentors from their rack,
tormented from their pain? By faith alone
your candles flicker on the railway track.

We stood behind the wire and watched them stack
our people into piles of earth and stone.
We are their ghosts, O do not call us back.

This station of the cross is draped in black.
Against our griefs the winter winds have blown.
Your candles flicker on the railway track.
We are their ghosts, O do not call us back.

Susan Skinner

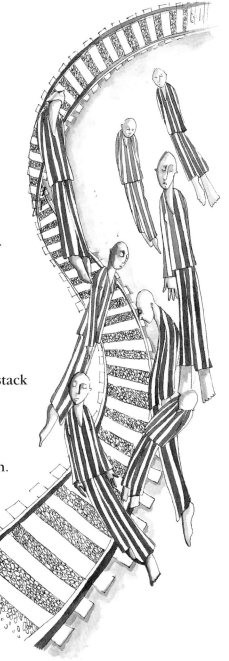

THE HERO

'Jack fell as he'd have wished,' the Mother said,
And folded up the letter that she'd read.
'The Colonel writes so nicely.' Something broke
In the tired voice that quavered to a choke.
She half looked up. 'We mothers are so proud
Of our dead soldiers.' Then her face was bowed.

Quietly the Brother Officer went out.
He'd told the poor old dear some gallant lies
That she would nourish all her days, no doubt.
For while he coughed and mumbled, her weak eyes
Had shone with gentle triumph, brimmed with joy,
Because he'd been so brave, her glorious boy.

He thought how 'Jack', cold-footed, useless swine,
Had panicked down the trench that night the mine
Went up at Wicked Corner; how he'd tried
To get sent home, and how, at last, he died,
Blown to small bits. And no one seemed to care
Except that lonely woman with white hair.

Siegfried Sassoon

THE RIGHTEOUS MOTHER

'Wretch!' cried the mother to her infant son.
'You hateful little boy, what have you done?
Killed the white butterfly, of all dear things,
And then pulled off his tiny, fairy wings.
To butterflies this garden is their home -
Here do they dance and kiss the flowers and roam
In happiness and plenty, even as you.
God would be very angry if He knew!'
And while she spoke these salutary words
Her hat displayed two withered humming-birds.

Eden Philpotts

WE ARE GOING TO SEE THE RABBIT

We are going to see the rabbit.
We are going to see the rabbit.
Which rabbit, people say?
Which rabbit, ask the children?
Which rabbit?
The only rabbit,
The only rabbit in England,
Sitting behind a barbed-wire fence
Under the floodlights, neon lights,
Sodium lights,
Nibbling grass
On the only patch of grass
In England, in England
(Except the grass by the hoardings
Which doesn't count.)
We are going to see the rabbit
And we must be there on time.

First we shall go by escalator,
Then we shall go by underground,
And then we shall go by motorway
And then by helicopterway,
And the last ten yards we shall have to go
On foot.

And now we are going
All the way to see the rabbit,
We are nearly there,
We are longing to see it,
And so is the crowd
Which is here in thousands

With mounted policemen
And big loudspeakers
And bands and banners,
And everyone has come a long way.
But soon we shall see it
Sitting and nibbling
The blades of grass
On the only patch of grass
In - but something has gone wrong!
Why is everyone so angry,
Why is everyone jostling
And slanging and complaining?

The rabbit has gone,
Yes, the rabbit has gone.
He has actually burrowed down into the earth
And made himself a warren, under the earth,
Despite all these people.
And what shall we do?
What can we do?

It is all a pity, you must be disappointed,
Go home and do something else for today,
Go home again, go home for today.
For you cannot hear the rabbit, under the earth,
Remarking rather sadly to himself, by himself,
As he rests in his warren, under the earth:
'It won't be long, they are bound to come,
They are bound to come and find me, even here.'

Alan Brownjohn

FIFTEEN MILLION PLASTIC BAGS

I was walking in a government warehouse
Where the daylight never goes
I saw fifteen million plastic bags
Hanging in a thousand rows.

Five million bags were six feet long
Five million bags were five foot five
Five million were stamped with Mickey Mouse
And they came in a smaller size.

Were they for guns or uniforms
Or a dirty kind of party game?
Then I saw each bag had a number
And every bag bore a name.

And five million bags were six feet long
Five million were five foot five
Five million were stamped with Mickey Mouse
And they came in a smaller size.

So I've taken my bag from the hanger
And I've pulled it over my head
And I'll wait for the priest to zip it
So the radiation won't spread.

Now five million bags are six feet long
Five million are five foot five
Five million are stamped with Mickey Mouse
And they came in a smaller size.

Adrian Mitchell

BEHIND THE STORY

'He must have been doing eighty up behind,'
The old man says. 'I couldn't get out of the way.'
'A bee hit me smack in the eye. I was blind,'
Is all the leathered, zippered youth can say.
'I couldn't see this joker round the bend.'

The girl who once had been a passenger
Lies on the grass under a coat, not caring,
Suddenly dead. Nearby, a part of her,
Still in the bloody shoe she had been wearing,
Begins to cool. It will be looked for later.

The old man simply stands. The back of his car
Is concave now, the window dark and yawning.
He vaguely wonders where his glasses are,
Why the worst horrors always give least warning,
Hears something somewhere dripping on hot tar.

'If this old devil hadn't been bloody crawling
I'd probably have missed him.' Now excuses
Come to the young imagination, falling
Out of the desperate air; these the tongue uses,
Trying to minimize, cushion the appalling.

.The dazed old man says nothing; watches sadly
While measurements are taken; wonders why
Accidents happen. He was not driving badly!
Unfair as it is he cannot ever deny
His thirty made the youth's shrill eighty deadly.

They will cart her off to a slab, the girl who is dead -
Her and the part of her - and attempt to make
The face presentable to be identified.
Next week the youth will talk of a new bike;
Brash again, say to his cronies, 'That old sod
Was too old to drive. He shouldn't be on the road.'

Eric Millward

SUMMER SOLSTICE, NEW YORK CITY

By the end of the longest day of the year he
could not stand it,
he went up the iron stairs through the roof of
the building
and over the soft, tarry surface
to the edge, put one leg over the complex
green tin cornice
and said if they came a step closer that was it.
Then the huge machinery of the earth began to
work for his life,
the cops came in their suits blue-grey as the sky
on a cloudy evening,
and one put on a bullet-proof vest, a
black shell around his own life,
life of his children's father, in case
the man was armed, and one, slung with a
rope like the sign of his bounden duty,
came up out of a hole in the top of the
neighbouring building
like the gold hole they say is in the top of the
head,
and began to lurk toward the man who wanted
to die.
The tallest cop approached him directly,
softly, slowly, talking to him, talking, talking,
while the man's leg hung over the lip of the
next world
and the crowd gathered in the street, silent,
and the
hairy net with its implacable grid was
unfolded near the curb and spread out and

stretched as the sheet is prepared to receive at a birth.
Then they all came a little closer
where he squatted next to his death, his shirt
glowing its milky glow like something
growing in a dish at night in the dark in a lab and then
everything stopped
as his body jerked and he
stepped down from the parapet and went toward them
and they closed on him. I thought they were going to
beat him up, as a mother whose child had been
lost will scream at the child when it's found, they
took him by the arms and held him up and leaned him against the wall of the
chimney and the
tall cop lit a cigarette
in his own mouth, and gave it to him, and
then they all lit cigarettes, and the
red, glowing ends burned like the
tiny campfires we lit at night
back at the beginning of the world.

Sharon Olds

SHOPPING TROLLEYS

notice how they have perfect steering
until you put something in them

their automatic response is to apply the brakes.
however they can be goaded forward

by the application of a foot sharply placed
on the rear bottom bar. surprise is essential

you can make them move their wheels
but there is no guarantee that they will all move

in the same direction. the poor things
are terrified & only want to escape. an average

family shopping turns them into nervous
wrecks for weeks. you might think that those

trolleys you see out in carparks & under
sapling trees are sight-seeing. they aren't.

they're trying to avoid having things put in them.
it's hopeless. there's always someone who wants

to use them as garbage bins laundry baskets
billy carts or flower pots. or bassinettes.

they are prolific breeders in the wild
& run in enormous herds

they rust in captivity & frequently collapse
during use. recovery is unusual.

Jenny Boult

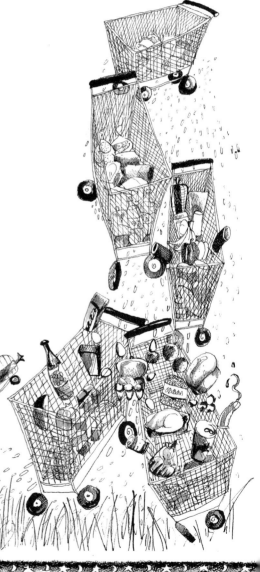

TULIPS ON THE ROUNDABOUT

The tulips stand where nobody goes
On the roundabout between the roads,
Some with yellow turbans on their heads
And some with red.
One road goes to the works
And one to school,
One under the railway bridge
And one to the swimming pool.
Peeping and screeching, the cars go past
The tulips in their turbans on the grass
That never seem to notice
The lorries rumbling round
But stand quite still
On their special piece of ground,
As if they had flown through the air
On a green magic carpet
And landed there.

Stanley Cook

HIGH STREET SMELLS

A busy street is a public library of smells -
the coffee grinder's fresh aroma at the corner,
the baker's sweet, buttery perfume -
you can almost taste the rolls, the pastries,
and drink the toasted coffee on the morning air.

Out of the sweet shops and the candy stores
oozes the exotic scent of marzipan and chocolate,
and the plebeian breath of chewing gum and
        gobstoppers.
The fruit market is a pungent orchard of
        essential juices.
and my ever-wary nose tells me that I'm approaching
the butcher's, with its plain whiffs of blood and
        sawdust,
while the sea itself comes swimming right
        across the pavement
as I pass the fishmonger's briny bouquets in ice
        and salt.

The Chinese takeaway, the Indian curry restaurant,
the fish-and-chip shop, McDonald's (smell is flavour),
the Olde Worlde Teashoppe, all have their
        distinctive auras
and tangs of sweet and sour, poppadums and spice,
deep-frying oil with vinegar. And toast, cakes
        and tea.

A gush of ironing steam from the laundry. The
        dry cleaner's
sharp, stinging reek, like smelling-salts - what
        a pong!

The pubs are open books of beer, wines and spirits
that my nostrils read rapidly, a kind of boozy braille.
The shoe emporium's rich emanations of supple
     leather, new shoes
impregnating the shoe boxes' pure white
     cardboard and tissue paper.
And here's the newsagent's - you can almost
     read the acrid print
of the local weekly, 'The Farming World',
     'The People's Friend',
'Popular Gardening', and all the comics before
     you even open them!

The voluptuous tobacconist's censes with its
     musky leaf
an entire shopping-mall - the drums, cartons
     and boxes
of honeyed shag, and tins of teasing snuff.

These are just some of the olfactory treats
for the aware nostril, the adventurous nose
seeking, among the banal stink and stench of
exhaust fumes.
the characters, the eccentrics, the silent friends
that are the original fragrances of busy streets.

_____
James Kirkup

ON LORD ILA'S IMPROVEMENTS, NEAR HOUNSLOW HEATH

Old Ila, to show his fine delicate taste
In improving his gardens purloined from the waste,
Bid his gard'ner one day to open his views,
By cutting a couple of grand avenues.
No particular prospect his Lordship intended,
But left it to chance how his walks should be ended,
With transports of joy he beheld at one view-end
His favourite prospect, a church that was ruined.
But, alas! What a sight did the next view exhibit
At the end of the walk hung a rogue on a gibbet.
He beheld it and wept, for it caused him to muse on
Full many a Campbell that died with his shoes on.
All amazed and aghast at the ominous scene
He ordered it quick to be closed up again
With a clump of Scotch firs by way of a screen.

Philip Stanhope, Earl of Chesterfield

THE CITY PEOPLE MEET THEMSELVES

The city people meet themselves
as they stare in the mirror of the opposite seat.
An old woman smiles at her reflection -
a girl, who's late for work
and urges the train on with a tapping foot -
the crumpled old woman remembers when
her feet tapped to speed up life
but now the feet are tired and old
and each step aches with dwindling hours;
a starched commuter tries not to look
at the broken-down man who cries -
his shallow eyes, pools of hopelessness,
the business man prays that life will be kind
and the treadmill of time will not leave him to cry
in the loneliness of a busy train;
an eager boy gapes at his reflection,
a huge man whose long arms reach to the straps
and smothers the boy in an aura of greatness -
the boy longs for the distant time
when his arms will reach
into the unknown realms of adulthood;
a worn out mother stares across
and sees another woman with the same gaze
grateful for child, but mournful for freedom.
Their eyes meet in silent conversation.

Rosanne Flynn   (Aged 14)

LONDON

I wander through each chartered street,
Near where the chartered Thames does flow,
And mark in every face I meet
Marks of weakness, marks of woe.

In every cry of every man,
In every infant's cry of fear,
In every voice, in every ban,
The mind-forged manacles I hear.

How the chimney-sweeper's cry
Every blackening church appalls;
And the hapless soldier's sigh
Runs in blood down palace walls.

But most through midnight streets I hear
How the youthful harlot's curse
Blasts the newborn infant's tear,
And blights with plagues the marriage hearse.

William Blake

THE JEELY PIECE SONG

I'm a skyscraper wean; I live on the nineteenth flair,
But I'm no gaun oot tae play ony mair,
'Cause since we moved tae Castlemilk, I'm wastin' away
'Cause I'm gettin' wan meal less every day:

    Oh ye cannae fling pieces oot a twenty storey flat,
    Seven hundred hungry weans'll testify to that.
    If it's butter, cheese or jeely, if the breid is plain or pan,
    The odds against it reaching earth are ninety-nine tae wan.

On the first day ma maw flung oot a daud o' Hovis broon;
It came skytin' oot the windae and went up insteid o' doon.
Noo every twenty-seven hoors it comes back intae sight
'Cause ma apiece went intae orbit and became a satellite.

On the second day ma maw flung me a piece oot wance again.
It went and hut the pilot in a fast low-flying plane.
He scraped it aff his goggles, shouting through the intercom,
'The Clydeside Reds huv goat me wi' a breid-an-jeely bomb.'

On the third day ma maw thought she would try another throw.
The Salvation Army band was staunin' doon below.
'Onward, Christian Soldiers' was the piece they should've played
But the oompah man was playing a piece an' marmalade.

We've wrote away to Oxfam to try an' get some aid,
An' a' the weans in Castlemilk have formed a 'piece brigade'.
We're gonnae march to George's Square demanding civil rights
Like nae mair hooses ower piece-flinging height.

Adam McNaughtan

DOWN AND OUT, PADDINGTON STATION

Weighed down by paper bags
And tired string-tied coat
She shuffled among the tables
Inspecting the abandoned drinks
Then sat and dozed the timetable away
The faded hair told nothing
Above the lines of ingrained dirt
She had a little time
Before the midnight deadline
We did not know her destination -
Perhaps a doorway in the Euston Road
The cheerful flowers mocked her
Watched by unseeing
Sleeping the sleep of the unloved.

Christine Boothroyd

DECOMPOSITION

I have a picture I took in Bombay
of a beggar asleep on the pavement:
grey-haired, wearing shorts and a dirty shirt,
his shadow thrown aside like a blanket.

His arms and legs could be cracks in the stone;
routes for the ants' journeys, the flies' descents.
brain-washed by the sun into exhaustion,
he lies veined into stone, a fossil man.

Behind him, there is a crowd passingly
bemused by a pavement trickster and quite
indifferent to this very common sight
of an old man asleep on the pavement.

I thought it then a good composition
and glibly called it The Man in the Street,
remarking how typical it was of
India that the man in the street lived there.

His head in the posture of one weeping
into a pillow chides me now for my
presumption at attempting to compose
art out of his hunger and solitude.

_____

Zulfikar Ghose

STREET BOY

Just you look at me, man,
Stompin' down the street
My crombie's stuffed with biceps
My boots is filled with feet.

Just you hark to me, man,
When they call us out
My head is full of silence
My mouth is full of shout.

Just you watch me move, man,
Steady like a clock
My heart is spaced on blue beat
My soul is toned on rock.

Just you read my name, man,
Writ for all to see
The walls is red with stories
The streets is filled with me.

Gareth Owen

CLOWN

He was safe
behind the whitened face
and red nose of his trade,
vocation more certain
than doctor's or priest's
to cheer and heal.
Hidden away from himself
he could always make us laugh
turning troubles like jackets
inside out, wearing
our rents and patches.

Tripping up in trousers too long
he made us feel tall;
and when we watched him
cutting himself down,
missing the ball,
we knew we could cope.
What we never knew
was the tightrope he walked
when the laughter had died.
Nowhere to hide in the empty night,
no one to catch his fall.

Phoebe Hesketh

FOODLESS CHILDREN

Foodless Children,
With stomachs puffed out,
Why have you no food to eat?
Why do you beg?

Foodless Children,
Suffering from starvation,
Why is your skin like paper?
Why do your bones poke out?

Foodless Children,
Eaten up by disease,
Why not see a doctor?
Why not?

Foodless Children,
You are so thin,
Your eyes are so appealing,
And you will soon be dead.

Maldwyn Davies

TRAVELLING CHILD

He came in tabby September
When the fair shrieked on the hill,
Stood on the classroom threshold,
Stray cat on our window-sill.

His gold eyes begged for a welcome,
For milk and a place at our fire
But his thin frame remembered overarm stones,
Claws that tore like barbed-wire.

In the yard after milk, in chrysanthemum sun,
We watched, domestic as cream.
The gipsy-boy, single, stood clenched by the fence,
Dark as a midnight dream.

We did not claw, nor spit nor hiss,
Yet we never invited him in,
Closed all our windows to with a thud,
Slammed each of our doors on him.

Jacqueline Brown

CIVIL LIES

Dear Teacher,

When I was born in Ethiopia
Life began,
As I sailed down the Nile civilization began,
When I stopped to think universities were built,
When I set sail
Asians and true Americans sailed with me.

When we traded nations were built,
We did not have animals,
Animals lived with us,
We had so much time
Thirteen months made our year,
We created social services
And cities that still stand.

So teacher do not say
Colombus discovered me
Check the great things I was doing
Before I suffered slavery.

Yours truly,

        Mr Africa

Benjamin Zephaniah

BLACKNESS

Blackness is me,
For I am black.
What mundane pow'r can change that fact?
If I should roam the world afar;
If I should soar the heights of stars;
If earthly honours I attract,
I'd still be black -
For black is black
And there is naught can change that fact.
Africa's my mother's name;
And it is she from whence I came.
That's why I'm black,
For so is she.
Blackness is our identity.
Blackness is what we want to be.
You are white;
Whiteness is you.
My Africa is not your mother,
But yet you are - you are my brother!

Glyne Walrond

SKIN

Teacher says I have many colours in my skin.
Some colours are thick. Some colours are thin.
I have a bit of everything mixed in …
browns, whites, blacks, pinks too
some of my veins are a greeny blue.
Teacher said it is a sad fact
that so many people only ever see black.

Pauline Stewart

CIRCLES

The white man drew a small circle in the sand
    and told the red man,
    'This is what the Indian knows,'
    and drawing a big circle around the small one,
    'This is what the white man knows.'

The Indian took the stick
    and swept an immense ring around both circles:
    'This is where the white man and the red man
    know nothing.'

Carl Sandberg

OUR ALLOTMENT

They often say 'Here is not like over there.'
My parents, who remember
when they were so much younger
tending their ground, planting a tree
hearing the wind in the sugar cane
sounding like sea.

'Here is not like over there,
here is quick, quick, there is slow.'
Except in the winter when frost and snow
keep us indoors,
avoiding all our gardening chores.

But in the spring they like it here
when flowers are opening everywhere.
Then they, with more enjoyment,
take extra pride in the allotment.

Even when they have grown grey hair
they'll still say, 'Here is not like over there.'
Over there they would have a few flying fish
to put with the potates which they call 'irish'
and also they would serve dasheen and yam
vegetables more common in their homeland.
They say the earth there smells of rust
that certain plants are poisonous but
me I have never been
across to see what they have seen
so I make do until I do with digging our allotment.

Pauline Stewart

SLEEPING COMPARTMENT

I don't like this, being carried sideways
through the night. I feel wrong and helpless - like
a timber broadside in a fast stream.

Such a way of moving may suit
that odd snake the sidewinder
in Arizona: but not me in Perthshire.

I feel at right angles to everything,
a cross grain in existence. - It scrapes
the top of my head, my footsoles.

To forget outside is no help either -
then I become a blockage
in the long gut of the train.

I try to think I am a through-the-looking-glass
mountaineer bivouacked
in a ledge five feet high.

It's no good. I go sidelong.
I rock sideways ... I draw in my feet
to let Aviemore pass.

Norman MacCaig

HOT AIR BALLOON

Here Be Dragons.   Old maps bred them, just too far
away to catch or tame, of course. But what comes here:

over the trees with a gravelly huff, half sign, half roar,
and a prickle of flame? I drop my book and stare

as it shoulders the sun aside. It settles, slow
as an eclipse, a candy-striped Big Top, hushed now

but for a creak of tackle, wind-hum in the wires …
The awning sags; its crate of precious wares,

half tiger cage, half laundry basket, thuds down,
spilling a figure out like dice across the lawn.

He finds his feet, dusts his greatcoat, wraps his scarf
twice round, squares his sideburns and his sad moustache,

and strides towards me, tipsy-brisk, as if uncertain
which of us is Stanley, which is Dr Livingstone.

He does not have to speak. I know where he has been -
over glassy deserts, jungles steaming in the sun,

peevish oceans, to the limits, to the outer regions
where the maps go blank, and men dream dragons,

anything, to fill the awful void of Do-Not-Know
that drifts in, endless, indescribable, like snow.

Philip Gross

THE TOURISTS

The tourists were a race of gods
(in shorts and crisp straw-hats)
awash with cash and slick kodaks
and, sometimes, baseball bats! ...

Their children trailed fat golden dolls,
that *spoke* and blinked their eyes,
and model planes that purred and *flew!* ... ...
(Some men called tourists "spies"!)

And *we*, the sun-daubed children, stood
with envy in our stare
at toys and joys white children had,
and deemed the world unfair!

But when we slept and were sliding down
moon rays and bright sunbeams,
we saw those children, pale and sad,
and bade them share our dreams!

Riad Nourallah

ROMANCE

When I was but thirteen or so
I went into a golden land
Chimborazo, Cotopaxi
Took me by the hand...

My father died, my brother too,
They passed like fleeting dreams,
I stood where Popocatepetl
In the sunlight gleams.

I dimly heard the master's voice
And boys far-off at play,
Chimborazo, Cotopaxi
had stolen me away.

I walked in a great golden dream
To and fro from school -
Shining Popocatepetl
The dusty streets did rule.

I walked home with a gold dark boy
And never a word I'd say,
Chimborazo, Cotopaxi
Had taken my speech away:

I gazed entranced upon his face
Fairer than any flower -
shining Popocatepetl
It was thy magic hour:

The houses, people, traffic seemed
Thin fading dreams by day,
Chimborazo, Cotopaxi
They had stolen my soul away!

J. Turner

IN MRS TILSCHER'S CLASS

You could travel up the Blue Nile
with your finger, tracing the route
while Mrs Tilscher chanted the scenery.
Tana. Ethiopia. Khartoum. Aswan.
That for an hour, then a skittle of milk
and the chalky Pyramids rubbed into dust.
A window opened with a long pole.
The laugh of a bell swung by a running child.

This was better than home. Enthralling books.
The classroom glowed like a sweet shop.
Sugar paper. Coloured shapes. Brady and Hindley
faded, like the faint, uneasy smudge of a mistake.
Mrs Tilscher loved you. Some mornings, you found
she'd left a good gold star by your name.
The scent of a pencil slowly, carefully, shaved.
A xylophone's nonsense heard from another form.

Over the Easter term, the inky tadpoles changed
from commas into exclamation marks. Three frogs
hopped in the playground, freed by a dunce,
followed by a line of kids, jumping and croaking
away from the lunch queue. A rough boy
told you how you were born. You kicked him, but stared
at your parents, appalled, when you got back home.

That feverish July, the air tasted of electricity.
A tangible alarm made you always untidy, hot,
fractious under the heavy, sexy sky. You asked her
how you were born and Mrs Tilscher smiled,
then turned away. Reports were handed out.
You ran through the gates, impatient to be grown,
as the sky split open into a thunderstorm.

Carol Ann Duffy

AN ACCIDENT

The playground noise stilled.
A teacher ran to the spot
beneath the climbing frame
where Rawinda lay, motionless.
We crowded around, silent,
gazing at the trickle of blood
oozing its way onto the tarmac.
Red-faced, the teacher shouted,
'move back ... get out of the way!'
and carried Rawinda into school,
limbs floppy as a rag doll's,
a red gash on her black face.

Later we heard she was at home,
five stitches in her forehead.
After school that day
Jane and I stopped beside the frame
and stared at the dark stain
shaped like a map of Ireland.
'Doesn't look much like blood,'
muttered Jane. I shrugged,
and remember now how warm it was
that afternoon, the white clouds,
and how sunlight glinted
from the polished bars.

We took Rawinda's 'Get Well' card
to her house. She was in bed,
quiet, propped up on pillows,
a white plaster on her dark skin.
Three days later
she was back at school,
her usual self, laughing,

twirling expertly on the bars,
wearing her plaster with pride,
covering for a week the scar
she would keep for ever,
memento of a July day at school.

Wes Magee

UNIFORM

'You'll grow,' she said and that was that. No use
To argue and to sulk invited slaps.
The empty shoulders drooped, the sleeves hung loose -
No use - she nods and the assistant wraps.

New blazer, new school socks and all between
Designed for pea pod anonymity.
All underwear the regulation green;
Alike there's none to envy, none to pity.

At home she feasts on pins. She tacks and tucks
Takes in the generous seams and smiles at thrift.
I fidget as she fits. She tuts and clucks.
With each neat stitch she digs a deeper rift.

They'll mock me with her turnings and her hem
And laugh and know that I'm not one of them.

Jan Dean

THE BOY WHO ATE HIS SANDWICHES TOO EARLY WHILE ON THE SCHOOL TRIP

'ANTHONY WRIGGLY!' boomed the teacher,
'I expect you think you're going
to win an early eater's medal
for having eaten all your sandwiches
by half-past ten. But I am not impressed.
Sandwiches are for lunch which is at 1 p.m.'

'But it's already 3.30 in Rawalpindi,' said Anthony,
his mouth full of the final piece of soggy crust.

'But we are not in Rawalpindi, Anthony,' replied the teacher,
    suppressing a sigh.
'We are in Norwich cathedral.'

'Well I'm not in that family over there,' said Anthony,
leaping towards a group of complete strangers
and pulling a gruesome face just as they were having
their photo taken,
'but I'll be in their holiday snaps!'

Lindsay MacRae

COMING LATE

Isabel comes late to school.
Tight as a bud in winter
into herself she curls
when our teacher reprimands her.

You are a slack and lazy girl.
You won't be any good …
(The voice has risen to a howl
of wind above a frozen wood)

… until you learn to come on time
and take more pride and show you care.
Isabel hides a living pain
beneath her blank and frosted stare.

She cannot say her dad has gone,
her mum is ill, she has to dress
and feed her brother, copes alone
without complaint; will not confess

her courage in a shrivelled life,
will not admit to anyone
that deep inside her is a fragile leaf
craving some warmth to open into sun.

Barrie Wade

SLOW JEANIE

There is this girl in my class called Jeanie.
She doesn't play with anybody much.
She is still on early readers.
Sometimes she does good pictures,
but she is not careful.
Sometimes she wears the same jumper for days,
even though it is dirty.
Sometimes she cries in dinners,
even though she is not a little one.
Nobody came to see her in the play,
even though she was Mrs. Noah,
and she saw the rainbow first.
At the end of school we run out of the gate like marbles,
but slow Jeanie creeps home in inches.

Rowena Sommerville

REMEMBER ME?

Remember me?
I am the boy who sought friendship;
The boy you turned away.
I the boy who asked you
If I too might play.
The face at the window
When your party was inside,
I the lonely figure
That walked away and cried.
I the one who hung around
A punchbag for your games.
Someone you could kick and beat,
Someone to call names.
But how strange is the change
After time has hurried by,
Four years have passed since then
Now I'm not so quick to cry.
I'm bigger and I'm stronger,
I've grown a foot in height,
Suddenly I'M popular
And YOU'RE left out the light.
I could, if I wanted,
Be so unkind to you.
I would only have to say
And the other boys would do.
But the memory of my pain
Holds back the revenge I'd planned
And instead, I feel much stronger
By offering you my hand.

Ray Mather

AN IMPERIAL EDUCATION

The P. & O. liner docked in Tilbury
and I who'd been looking for Wordsworth's landscapes
(since the old Empire still educated the new India)
saw instead the blurred shapes
of a wet April day: a drear
England appeared of cranes, warehouses and silvery

railway tracks. At London
Bridge, I leaned over the murky, embittered
Thames, taking an old-fashioned Eng. Lit. view,
not seeing the littered
river but some dew-
drenched willow branches hanging over a sylvan

stream a Blackie textbook
had made me long for in a Bombay classroom.
I walked the streets of London with a pensive
face, a posture assumed
from some page in *Palgrave*
or a Millais reproduction, calculated to look

similar to the shepherds
returning from the meadows of their offices
to the bedsitting cottages in South Ken.
All my suits were three-piece
pinstripe with a red carnation
in the buttonhole. Swallows were all the birds

I saw, daffodils all
the flowers. I wouldn't drink beer because I'd
been told that young men only drank sherry.
A Byron from Bombay, I sighed,
looked sad and world-weary.
Peter Sellers' Indian was less comical

than my rendering
of English customs. The naïve, confused
and clueless East died slowly. Imitative
    and sycophantic, used
        to a century of submissive
bowing, the Indian, always when *God Save the King*

    was played, stood more erect
than the Englishman. That and Macaulay
were my education, Now I wonder what immigrants
    arriving in Southall say
        about their long acquaintance
with the English way of life which they must suspect

    of a subtle corruption,
being run by Fagins and Artful Dodgers. Well,
dear English reader, know that whether it's Delhi's
    sudden dismissal
        of the B.B.C., or Shelley's
words in my mouth, it's all due to Imperial Education.

Zulfikar Ghose

TALL WINDOWS

Jimmy Pask stares through our tallest windows,
as if his gaze could win escape from tests
of spelling. Miss wonders where his mind goes
when his eyes turn downy as a songbird's nest.

It's on the hottest days they come,
when sunshine fills their eyes or heat
baffles their brains; then the classroom
windows stop them in their tracks, swat

them down like gnats from rash speedways
along heady currents. The crack
of beak on glass rattles the glaze
of our tall windows, sets us back

in sorrow, since we cannot rest
until we see the face of death
or put our faint, fluttering hope to test.
We do not need to hold our breath

for long. Jimmy Pask returns
with the shoebox coffin he keeps
specially for the purpose. He learns
fast about birds and never weeps

like some of us about their brittle
lives. This one's a snap-necked songthrush.
Jimmy lets us stroke the little
speckles that seem still warm to touch,

before he shuts the lid. Miss Law
will let him bury it at break
as usual. She trusts him more
with this than with his reading book,

but Jim is good with birds. He lets
one of the girls write SONGTHRUSH neat
and bold upon the lid, regrets
he can't perform this simple rite.

I watch him trace the mystery
of letters, seeking patterns pressed
as definite as flecks of glory
fledged on ruffled wing or stippled breast.

Barrie Wade

THE BULLY ASLEEP

This afternoon, when grassy
Scents through the classroom crept,
Bill Craddock laid his head
Down on his desk, and slept.

The children came round him:
Jimmy, Roger, and Jane;
They lifted his head timidly
And let it sink again.

'Look, he's gone sound asleep, Miss,'
Said Jimmy Adair;
'He stays up all night, you see;
His mother doesn't care.'

'Stand away from him children.'
Miss Andrews stooped to see.
'Yes, he's asleep; go on
With your writing, and let him be.'

'Now's a good chance!' whispered Jimmy,
And he snatched Bill's pen and hid it.
'Kick him under the desk, hard;
He won't know who did it.'

'Fill all his pockets with rubbish -
Paper, apple-cores, chalk.'
So they plotted, while Jane
Sat wide-eyed at their talk.

Not caring, not hearing,
Bill Craddock he slept on;
Lips parted, eyes closed -
Their cruelty gone.

'Stick him with pins!' muttered Roger.
'Ink down his neck!' said Jim.
But Jane, tearful and foolish,
Wanted to comfort him.

John Walsh

SUNSTRUCK

There's a pencil of light
On my bedroom rug;
It lies there so bright
I nearly picked it up.
When I put my finger on it
It warmed me to the bone.
I'd like to write with it
A letter of pure sunshine
But I've got to go to school now
And it won't be there when I
come home.

Darien Smith

BACK TO SCHOOL BLUES

Late August,
The miserable countdown starts,
Millions of kids
With lead in their hearts
In Woollies' window: rubbers, rulers,
Geometry sets,
And a BACK TO SCHOOL sign -
I mean, who forgets?
In the clothes shops
Ghastly models of kids with
New satchels and blazers and shoes:
Enough to give anybody
Those Back to School Blues.

And Auntie Nell from Liverpool,
Who's down with us for a visit,
Smiles and says, 'So it's back to school
On Wednesday for you is it?
I only wish I'd got the chance
Of my schooldays over again ...
Happiest days of my life they were -
Though I didn't realise it then ...'
And she rabbits on like that,
Just twisting away at the screws;
She's forgotten about
The Back to School Blues.

And six and a half long weeks
Have melted away like ice cream:
That Costs Brava fortnight's
Vanished like a dream.
And Dad says, 'Look, this term
At school, could you try and do
A bit better?
For a start you could learn to spell
And write a decent letter.
And just keep away from that Hazel Stephens -
She's total bad news.'
Any wonder that I've got
Those Back to School Blues?

Eric Finney

TO A TRAINEE ACCOUNTANT

You have traded your schooldesk for an office replica,
in two years time you will qualify - for what?
In four years you will marry
leaving your parents' home to buy a block of land
on which to place your square, orange brick home from home.
You will have three children, one motor car,
a twenty year mortgage and a weekly game of
cards with the people down the road.
On Saturday you will wash your car while listening to the football,
on Sunday mow the lawn and eat a barbecue lunch.
By fifty you will have left behind all aspirations dreams and hopes,
at sixty you will be made chief clerk - a man who is respected,
a man who is respectable,
a man to be listened to with nothing to say.
At sixty-five you will retire, a brief farewell speech,
a watch, a travelling rug and dinner on the company,
a clearing of desks and waving goodbyes,
and two weeks later someone will say,
'the place feels funny without old whatsisname,'
and no one there will ever think of you again.
Meanwhile you will go on that world trip,
to return, mind broadened, after a year
of ships, and buses, hotels and places where you mustn't drink
    the water.
Six months after returning you will die of
a boredom induced heart attack.
Fifty-two people will attend your funeral, and
return to their houses already thinking of other things,
your wife will knit socks for your grandchildren,
watch T.V., make cups of tea for the neighbours
and occasionally wonder what you were really like.

Michael Dugan

WARNING

When I am an old woman I shall wear purple
With a red hat which doesn't go, and doesn't suit me,
And I shall spend my pension on brandy and summer gloves
And satin sandals, and say we've no money for butter.
I shall sit down on the pavement when I'm tired
And gobble up samples in shops and press alarm bells
And run my stick along the public railings
And make up for the sobriety of my youth.
I shall go out in my slippers in the rain
And pick the flowers in other people's gardens
And learn to spit.

You can wear terrible shirts and grow more fat
And eat three pounds of sausages at a go
Or only bread and pickle for a week
And hoard pens and pencils and beermats and things in boxes.

But now we must have clothes that keep us dry
And pay the rent and not swear in the street
And set a good example for the children.
We must have friends to dinner and read the papers.

But maybe I ought to practise a little now?
So people who know me are not too shocked and surprised
When suddenly I am old and start to wear purple.

Jenny Joseph

FOR MY GRANDMOTHER KNITTING

There is no need they say
but the needles still move
their rhythms in the working of your hands
as easily
as if your hands
were once again those sure and skilful hands
of the fisher-girl.

You are old now
and your grasp of things is not so good
but master of your moments then
deft and swift
you slit the still-ticking quick silver fish.
Hard work it was too
of necessity.

But now they say there is no need
as the needles move
in the working of your hands
once the hands of the bride
with the hand-span waist
once the hands of the miner's wife
who scrubbed his back
in a tin bath by the coal fire
once the hands of the mother
of six who made do and mended
scraped and slaved slapped sometimes
when necessary.

But now they say there is no need
the kids they say grandma
have too much already
more than they can wear
too many scarves and cardigans -
gran you do too much
there's no necessity.
At your window you wave
them goodbye Sunday.
With your painful hands
big on shrunken wrists.
Swollen-jointed. Red. Arthritic. Old.
But the needles still move
their rhythms in the working of your hands
easily
as if your hands remembered
of their own accord the pattern
as if your hands had forgotten
how to stop.

_____

Liz Lochhead

SHED IN SPACE

My Grandad Lewis
On my mother's side
Had two ambitions.
One was to take first prize
For shallots at the village show
And the second
Was to be a space commander.
Every Tuesday
After I'd got their messages,
He'd lead me with a wink
To his garden shed
And there, amongst the linseed
And the sacks of peat and horse manure
He'd light his pipe
And settle in his deck chair.
His old eyes on the blue and distant
That no one else could see,
He'd ask,
'Are we A O.K. for lift off?'
Gripping the handles of the lawn mower
I'd reply:
'A O.K.'
And then
Facing the workbench,
In front of shelves of paint and creosote
And racks of glistening chisels.
He'd talk to Mission Control.
'Five - Four - Three - Two - One - Zero -
We have lift off.
This is Grandad Lewis talking,
Do you read me?
Britain's first space shed
is rising majestically into orbit

From its launch pad
In the allotments
In Lakey Lane.'
And so we'd fly,
Through timeless afternoons
Till tea time came,
Amongst the planets
And mysterious suns,
While the world
Receded like a dream:
Grandad never won
That prize for shallots,
But as the captain
Of an intergalactic shed
There was no one to touch him.

Gareth Owen

FOLLOWER

My father worked with a horse-plough,
His shoulders globed like a full sail strung
Between the shafts and the furrow.
The horses strained at his clicking tongue.

An expert. He would set the wing
And fit the bright steel-pointed sock.
The sod rolled over without breaking.
At the headrig, with a single pluck

Of reins, the sweating team turned round
And back into the land. His eye
Narrowed and angled at the ground,
Mapping the furrow exactly.

I stumbled in his hob-nailed wake,
Fell sometimes on the polished sod;
Sometimes he rode me on his back
Dipping and rising to his plod.

I wanted to grow up and plough,
To close one eye, stiffen my arm.
All I ever did was follow
In his broad shadow round the farm.

I was a nuisance, tripping, falling,
Yapping always. But today
It is my father who keeps stumbling
Behind me, and will not go away.

Seamus Heaney

THE ELEPHANT TABLE

Grandma boot-polished them
    glistening black -
four mahogany heads
facing north, south, east, west
    with a world on their back,

a world carved out whole
    from one slice of a tree,
a world that grew old
while the Viceroy asked princes
    to treaties and tea

and outside in the dust
    quiet lean watchful men
and their elephants waited
what seemed like an age
    for the party to end.

In Grandma's dark parlour
    I crouched eye to eye
with the south-facing elephant.
Where was it looking
    so weary, and why?

And what makes me reach back
    years later to feel
little-finger-sized tusks?
'Those are precious,' said Grandma.
    'They're real.'

Philip Gross

AS I WALKED OUT IN THE STREETS OF LAREDO

As I walked out in the streets of Laredo,
As I walked out in Laredo one day,
I spied a poor cowboy wrapped up in white linen,
Wrapped up in white linen as cold as the clay.

'I see by your outfit that you are a cowboy,'
These words he did say as I boldly stepped by.
'Come, sit down beside me and hear my sad story;
I was shot in the breast and I know I must die.

Once in my saddle I used to look handsome,
Once in my saddle I used to look gay.
I first went to drinkin' and then to card playin',
Got shot in the breast, which ended my day.

Let sixteen gamblers come handle my coffin,
Let sixteen girls come carry my pall;
Put bunches of roses all over my coffin,
Put roses to deaden the clods as they fall.

And beat the drums slowly and play the fife lowly,
And play the dead march as you carry me along;
Take me to the prairie and lay the sod o'er me,
For I'm a young cowboy and I know I've done wrong.'

We beat the drums slowly and played the fife lowly,
And bitterly wept as we bore him along;
For we all loved our comrade so brave, young and
    handsome,
We loved the young cowboy although he'd done wrong.

Anonymous

HOW DOES IT FEEL?

How does it feel?
OK All right.
How does it really feel?
OK All right.
But how does it really, really feel
without saying OK?

Yesterday my kitten died
and the oceans of my eyes
burst wide open. How's that?

David Scott

YELLOW

I stamped through the pastures
booting the heads off buttercups
I stormed in out of the wheatfield
into a country kitchen
and let out my gurrier roar:
'Yellah! Yellah! Yellah!'
But she took me on her knee
and said: no, it's yellow.
I glowed, I echoed yellow
but that was a colour
I had never seen
till I saw her stretched on a hospital bed
the yellow of cancer and nicotine.

Michael O'Loughlin

BALLAD OF BIRMINGHAM

'Mother dear, may I go downtown
instead of out to play,
and march the streets of Birmingham
in a freedom march today?'

'No, baby, no, you may not go,
for the dogs are fierce and wild,
and clubs and hoses, guns and jails
ain't good for a little child.'

'But, mother, I won't be alone.
Other children will go with me,
and march the streets of Birmingham
to make our country free.'

'No, baby, no, you may not go,
for I fear those guns will fire.
But you may go to church instead,
and sing in the children's choir.'

She has combed and brushed her nightdark hair,
and bathed rose-petal sweet,
and drawn white gloves on her small brown hands,
and white shoes on her feet.

The mother smiled to know her child
was in the sacred place,
but that smile was the last smile
to come upon her face.

For when she heard the explosion,
her eyes grew wet and wild.
She raced through the streets of Birmingham
calling for her child

She clawed through bits of glass and brick,
then lifted out a shoe.
'O, here's the shoe my baby wore,
but, baby, where are you?'

Dudley Randall

THE TWA CORBIES

As I was walking all alane,
I heard twa corbies making a mane:
The tane unto the tither did say,
'Whar sall we gang and dine the day?'

' - In behind yon auld fail dyke
I wot there lies a new-slain knight;
And naebody kens that he lies there
But his hawk, his hound, and his lady fair.

'His hound is to the hunting gane,
His hawk to fetch the wild-fowl hame,
His lady's ta'en anither mate,
So we may mak' our dinner sweet.

'Ye'll sit on his white hause-bane,
And I'll pick out his bonny blue e'en:
Wi'ae lock o' his gowden hair
We'll theek our nest when it grows bare.

'Mony a one for him maks mane,
But nane sall ken whar he is gane:
O'er his white banes, when they are bare,
The wind sall blaw for evermair.'

Anonymous

All the world's a stage,
And all the men and women merely players:
They have their exits and their entrances;
And one man in his time plays many parts,
His acts being seven ages. At first the infant,
Mewling and puking in the nurse's arms.
And then the whining school-boy, with his satchel
And shining morning face, creeping like a snail
Unwillingly to school. And then the lover,
Sighing like furnace, with a woeful ballad
Made to his mistress' eyebrow. Then a soldier,
Full of strange oaths, and bearded like the pard,
Jealous in honour, sudden and quick in quarrel,
Seeking the bubble reputation
Even in the cannon's mouth. And then the justice,
In fair round belly with good capon lin'd,
With eyes severe, and beard of formal cut,
Full of wise saws and modern instances;
And so he plays his part. The sixth age shifts
Into the lean and slipper'd pantaloon,
With spectacles on nose and pouch on side,
His youthful hose well sav'd, a world too wide
For his shrunk shank; and his big manly voice,
Turning again toward childish treble, pipes
And whistles in his sound. Last scene of all,
That ends this strange eventful history,
Is second childishness and mere oblivion,
Sans teeth, sans eyes, sans taste, sans everything.

William Shakespeare   *from As You Like It*

HOLY SONNET

Death, be not proud, though some have called thee
    Mighty and dreadful, for thou art not so;
    For those whom thou think'st though dost overthrow
Die not, poor Death, nor yet canst thou kill me.
From rest and sleep, which but thy pictures be,
    Much pleasure - then, from thee much more must flow;
    And soonest our best men with thee do go,
Rest of their bones and soul's delivery.
Thou'rt slave to fate, chance, kings and desperate men,
    And dost with poison, war, and sickness dwell;
    And poppy or charms can make us sleep as well,
And better than thy stroke. Why swell'st thou then?
    One short sleep past, we wake eternally,
    And death shall be no more. Death, thou shalt die.

John Donne

DAD

Two days before he died
My sister made a bed for him
In what they called his living room.
Too busy chasing every breath by now
The irony passed him by.
On the TV in the corner
Two ageing gunslingers
Challenged each other
To one last shoot-out
Before a paying audience
In the sand-strewn bullring.
"Winner takes all," snarled Kirk,
But what the winner takes, I thought,
Is what we all of us will get
If we wait unchallenged long enough.

They never said that in those
Happy Ever After films
We once were nourished on,
That always faded in impassioned kisses.
But in the streets outside
Hurrying homewards to our several lives
We soon find out the After's not for Ever
And even star-kissed lips
Dissolve to dust in Time.
Westerns he'd always liked
But this last one outlived him
So he never saw the final
Thundering shoot-out in the sun,
Nor heard the diapason swell
Above the closing titles
And the last dissolve.

Punctilious to the last,
Sensing an appointment to be kept,
He wound his watch a final time,
Told Anne he loved her,
Then composed himself until
The erratic knocking in his wrist
Gave up the ghost for good.
Someone opened a window
For his fleeing soul
And across the hills
The great and endless night
Came pouring in from everywhere.

Gareth Owen

LITTLE HOMER'S SLATE

After dear old grandma died,
 Hunting through an oaken chest
In the attic, we espied
 What repaid our childish quest;
'Twas a homely little slate,
Seemingly of ancient date.

On its quaint and battered face
 Was the picture of a cart,
Drawn with all that awkward grace
 Which betokens childish art;
But what meant this legend, pray:
"Homer drew this yesterday"?

Mother recollected then
 What the years were fain to hide -
She was but a baby when
 Little Homer lived and died;
Forty years, so mother said,
Little Homer had been dead.

This one secret through those years
 Grandma kept from all apart,
Hallowed by her lonely tears
 And the breaking of her heart;
While each year that sped away
Seemed to her but yesterday.

So the homely little slate
 Grandma's baby's fingers pressed,
To a memory consecrate,
 Lieth in the oaken chest,
Where, unwilling we should know,
Grandma put it, years ago.

Eugene Field

LEAVE-TAKING

The only joy
of his old age
he often said
was his grandson

Their friendship
straddled
eight decades
three generations

They laughed, played
quarrelled, embraced
watched television together
and while the rest had
little to say to the old man
the little fellow was
a fountain of endless chatter

When death rattled
the gate at five
one Sunday morning
took the old man away
others trumpeted their
grief in loud sobs
and lachrymose blubber

He never shed a tear
just waved one of his
small inimitable goodbyes
to his grandfather
and was sad the old man
could not return his gesture.

Cecil Rajendra

GRAVE OF A PRINCESS

Between the hills of Hindu Kush
and vale of Amu Darya
a princess lies in templed tomb
where tribesman worshipped fire,

where traders on the great Silk Route
paid tolls in precious stones,
in treasures from the Orient
which now surround her bones.

Her hollowed eyes stare from a skull
adorned with crown, collapsible -
like trees with leaves in flakes of gold
slipped in a headband - flat they'd fold
for, being a nomadic wife,
this suited well her way of life.
Once raven hair had been festooned
by pendants linked like mobile moons,

a necklace hewn from ivory,
pearl beads with hearts of turquoise,
a bracelet like an antelope
and sewn on shrouds around her loins

gold spangles, disks - and ancient coins
are showered like confetti.
Her fingers, ringed with treasures, clutch
at combs of ebony,
a Chinese mirror laid to rest
upon her jewel-encrusted breast,
a pot of silver filled with oils -
her beauty secrets sealed by coils
of serpent. Princess well prepared

for journeying lay undisturbed
for centuries. She's almost gone
to lands beyond Afghanistan.

Gina Douthwaite

REQUIESCAT

Tread lightly, she is near
    Under the snow,
Speak gently, she can hear
    The daisies grow.

All her bright golden hair
    Tarnished with rust,
She that was young and fair
    Fallen to dust.

Lily-like, white as snow,
    She hardly knew
She was a woman, so
    Sweetly she grew.

Coffin-board, heavy stone,
    Lie on her breast;
I vex my heart alone,
    She is at rest.

Peace, peace; she cannot hear
    Lyre or sonnet;
All my life's buried here.
    Heap earth upon it.

Oscar Wilde

WITH HER HEAD TUCKED UNDERNEATH HER ARM

In the Tower of London, large as life
The ghost of Ann Boleyn walks, they declare.
Poor Ann Boleyn was once King Henry's wife -
Until he made the Headsman bob her hair!
Ah yes! He did her wrong long years ago
And she comes up at night to tell him so.

With her head tucked underneath her arm
She walks the Bloody Tower!
With her head tucked underneath her arm
At the Midnight hour.
Along the draughty corridors for miles
and miles she goes,
She often catches cold, poor thing,
it's cold there when it blows,
And it's awfully awkward for the
Queen to have to blow her nose
With her head tucked
underneath her arm!

Sometimes gay King Henry gives a spread
For all his pals and gals - a ghostly crew.
The headsman carves the joint and cuts the bread,
Then in comes Ann Boleyn to 'queer' the 'do',
She holds her head up with a wild war whoop,
And Henry cries 'Don't drop it in the soup!'

With her head tucked underneath her arm
She walks the Bloody Tower!
With her head tucked underneath her arm
At the Midnight hour!

P. Weston and Bert Lee

REMEMBER

Remember me when I am gone away,
    Gone far away into the silent land;
    When you can no more hold me by the hand,
Nor I half turn to go yet turning stay.
Remember me when no more day by day
    You tell me of our future that you planned:
    Only remember me; you understand
It will be late to counsel then or pray.

Yet if you should forget me for a while
    And afterwards remember, do not grieve:
    For if the darkness and corruption leave
    A vestige of the thoughts that once I had,
Better by far you should forget and smile
    Than that you should remember and be sad.

Christina Rossetti

YOU NEVER SEE A BRIGHT YELLOW HEARSE

The English don't die they just become discreet
You never see a hearse clamped on Harley Street
Or parked at a picnic site
Near Lovers' Leap

You never see a hearse outside a betting shop
Left next to a row of prams
You never see the route to the cemetery
Served by special hearse trams

You never see a hearse at a wedding
Or on adverts for banks
Or a row of hearses at a military parade
Behind a squadron of tanks

Or outside a nightclub at closing time
With racing stripes down the bonnet
Or a hearse at the Motor Show
With dead models draped upon it

You never see a double-decker hearse
Or a hearse that's extra wide
Or a hearse with four or five coffins
All crammed up inside

You never see a coffin in a side car
For a fanatical ex-biker
Or a hearse at a transport café
Picking up a hitch-hiker

You never see a hearse used for ram-raiding
Or a hearse with fluffy dice
Or a hearse with a taxi meter
So you can keep an eye on the price

You never see a hearse at an auction
Some dealer's trying to flog
Or a hearse with a trailer
For someone who died with their dog

Each hearse is black and clean and neat
Because the English don't die they just become discreet.

Henry Normal

DIRGE FOR UNWIN

Uncle Unwin
lived unwed,
died unmourned,
our tears unshed,
his chin unshaved,
his soul unsaved,
his feet unwashed,
his cat unfed,

uncouth, unkempt,
no cuff unfrayed,
his floor unswept,
his bed unmade,
ungenerous,
unkind to us,
the undertaker's bill unpaid

until
his will,
found undercover,
  left untold wealth
      to an unknown lover.
        It's so unfair.
          We were unaware:
            even nobodies count
              on one another.

Philip Gross

ALL THAT SPACE

Great-grandad
used to tell me stories -
tales, he called them,
about when he was a lad

how he fled city streets
flew on his bike
down lanes between cornfields,
past Kenyon's Brick Works
to the Moss

sitting for hours
in all that space

played his mouth organ,
and watched ...
peewits wild violets silhouette
of chimneys against the sky

his shabby jersey, battered clogs, shamed
by new-moon-silver buds of willow,
baby-skin softness of dog-rose petal.

In the Home, carers try to interest him
in television, don't understand
when he turns his chair to the wall,
the print of Constable's Hay Wain,
curves his fingers round
his smiling mouth,
and tilts his head, listens ...
sitting for hours   in all that space.

Joan Poulson

DEATH BY SACHER TORTE

There's a churchyard in Vienna where
nine graves lie side by side by side.
A respected old Viennese Baker
and his full eight wives. The
old Baker was famous for his
wonderful chocolate cake,
for the puddings and the
strudel, and the pies
he could bake. Nobody
remembers them now
and you have to
peer very hard
at the graves
to read the
writing
that's
left:

The respected Viennese Baker, fed them all to death.

Elizabeth Seagar

WHEN I AM DEAD

When I am dead
Cry for me a little
Think of me sometimes
But not too much.
Think of me now and again
As I was in life
At some moments it's pleasant to recall
But not for long
Leave me in peace
And I shall leave you in peace
And while you live
Let your thoughts
be with the living.

Anonymous

ETERNAL LOVE

We both knew it was time for you to go
and I, with dread, would face the emptiness,
the unremitting loneliness,
the unrelenting end.
Your eyes gave me that one last look
of love
and - so it seemed - of something more.
Its meaning I could not then comprehend.

And so you left I thought for good
but still that look remained.
And it was then I understood.
This was not to be the end at all.

Your body may have gone, it's true.
But bodies change from day to day,
new cells reborn as old decay
Not so that inner self that makes you you,
That changeless self lives on, lives through.

The love we share,
much stronger than mere memory that fades,
goes on and grows and floods back in cascades
And overwhelmed, my very being dissolves
to merge with yours again.

You're with me
when the dewdrops glisten at tomorrow's dawn.
You're with me
when the sun's rays lift the veil of misty morn.
You're with me
when the thrushes greet the day with song.
I feel you at my side the whole day long.
When shadows lengthen
You're still at my side.

And when night falls
and sleep takes rein,
you're there, once more,
close to my heart again.

John Lacorte

DYING QUIETLY

These children die quietly;
No headlines screaming across the page,
No rage from politicians blaming others,
No mothers appearing on our screens,
Seen waving banners asking why
Did her child and forty thousand others die
Today.
The way they die is quietly,
Not for the want of a miracle cure;
Pure water, food, simple medications are all they're needing.
So proceedings will not be taken out;
Without a voice
No choice but to die
Unheard.
The words must come
From others.

Pat Moon

UP-HILL

Does the road wind up-hill all the way?
    Yes, to the very end.
Will the day's journey take the whole long day?
    From morn to night, my friend.

But is there for the night a resting-place?
    A roof for when the slow dark hours begin.
May not the darkness hide it from my face?
    You cannot miss that inn.

Shall I meet other wayfarers at night?
    Those who have gone before.
Then must I knock, or call when just in sight?
    They will not keep you standing at that door.

Shall I find comfort, travel-sore and weak?
    Of labour you shall find the sum.
Will there be beds for me and all who seek?
    Yea, beds for all who come.

Christina Rossetti

Our revels now are ended. These our actors,
As I foretold you, were all spirits and
Are melted into air, into thin air:
And, like the baseless fabric of this vision,
The cloud-capp'd towers, the gorgeous palaces,
The solemn temples, the great globe itself,
Yea, all which it inherit, shall dissolve
And, like this insubstantial pageant faded,
Leave not a rack behind. We are such stuff
As dreams are made on, and our little life
Is rounded with a sleep.

_____

William Shakespeare   from The Tempest

AUTHOR INDEX

THE LAW OF COPYRIGHT (AFTER KIPLING)

Now this is the Law of Copyright – a good
  subject for Poetry Day.
If you keep it some poets may prosper, in a
  modest and limited way.

And some of the people who break it have
  little idea of the wrong
They do to the indigent author who
  dreamed up the poem or song

That they put into print without asking, or
  perform in a theatre or hall
With an audience paying good money, while
  the writer gets nothing at all,

Or offer the world on their websites,
  assuming that poems are free.
They are shocked when you mention
  permission, aghast if there's talk of a fee.

This is the law: the creator has rights that
  you can't overlook.
It isn't OK to make copies – you have to
  fork out for the book.

It isn't OK to use poems on posters or
  cards or in shows
Unless you have asked for permission. You
  may have to pay through the nose

But not necessarily. Try it. If you're a good
  cause, or you're poor,
And unlikely to make any profit, the cost of
  obeying the law

May be negligible, may be nothing. It's one
  thing to ask for a gift
And another to take without asking, and we
  call that other thing theft.

And poets they need to eat supper, and
  poets they need to wear shoes
And you'll seldom encounter a poet
  enjoying a luxury cruise,

So remember the Law of Copyright, and
  make sure you do as you ought,
And if you read this and ignore it, I bloody
  well hope you get caught.

Wendy Cope

ACKNOWLEDGEMENTS

Opal Palmer Adisa: 'I Am the One' from *A Caribbean Dozen* © 1994 Opal Palmer Adisa, edited by John Agard and Grace Nichols. Reproduced by permission of the publisher Walker Books Ltd., London. **John Agard:** 'Poetry Jump Up'. By kind permission of John Agard c/o The Caroline Sheldon Literary Agency. First performed at the Brent Poetry Festival 1985. **Caroline Allen:** 'Richard'. From *Wondercrump 2* edited by Jennifer Curry. By permission of Random House. **Karina Bailey:** 'Dentist'. From *Wondercrump 3* edited by Jennifer Curry. By permission of Random House. **Wanda Barford:** 'Conversation with an Angel'. By permission of Faber and Faber.

Anne Bell: 'Milking Song'. By permission of Anne Bell. **James Berry:** 'Mum, Dad and Me'. Reprinted by permission of the Peters, Fraser and Dunlop Group on behalf of James Berry. © James Berry 1998. **Keith Bosley:** 'Door'. By permission of Keith Bosley from *And I Dance*, Angus and Robertson (UK) Ltd 1972. **Jacqueline Brown:** 'Have You Ever Thought', 'Travelling Child'. By permission of the Author, Jacqueline Brown. **Alan Brownjohn:** 'We are going to see the rabbit', 'Explorer'. © Alan Brownjohn. **Barry Buckingham:** 'The Great Sphinx By The Nile'. By permission of Barry Buckingham. **Charles Causley:** 'Green Man in the Garden', 'Family Feeling'. By permission of Charles Causley and Macmillan, from *Collected Poems*. **Stanley Cook:** 'Tulips on the Roundabout'. © the estate of Stanley Cook. **Wendy Cope:** 'The Law of Copyright (after Kipling)'. By permission of Wendy Cope. 'The Uncertainty of the Poet' from *Serious Concerns* reprinted by permission of Faber and Faber. **Sue Cowling:** 'Jeopardy' from *What is a Kumquat* reprinted by permission of Faber and Faber. **Roy Daniells:** 'Noah'. By permission of E Laurenda Daniells. **Berlie Doherty:** 'The Face at the Window'. By permission of Berlie Doherty. **Carol Ann Duffy:** 'In Mrs Tilscher's Class'. Reproduced by permission of the publishers Anvil Press Poetry Ltd. **Paul Durcan:** 'Tullynoe: Tete-a-Tete in the Parish Priest's Parlour', taken from the collection *A Snail in My Prime*, first published by The Harvill Press in 1993. Copyright Paul Durcan 1993. Reproduced by permission of the Harvill Press. **Max Fatchen:** 'Be Nice to Rhubarb' reproduced by permission of The John Johnson Agency. **Eric Finney:** 'Back to School Blues'. By permission of Eric Finney. **Robert Fisher:** 'Monster Alphabet'. By permission of Robert Fisher. **Rosanne Flynn:** 'The City People Meet Themselves'. From *Wondercrump 1* edited by Jennifer Curry. By permission of Random House. **Kim Garrard:** 'The Sculptor' From *Wondercrump 2* edited by Jennifer Curry. By permission of Random House. **Zulfikar Ghose:** 'Decomposition'. © 1967 by Zulfikar Ghose, first published in *Jets From Orange* Macmillan, London. 'An Imperial Education'. © 1972 Zulfikar Ghose first published in *The Violent West*, Macmillan. **Robert Graves:** 'The Alice Jean' by Robert Graves from *Collected Poems* reprinted by permission of Faber and Faber. **Philip Gross:** 'The Elephant Table'. 'Hot Air Balloon' from *Manifold Manor* reprinted by permission of Faber and Faber. 'Dirge for Unwin' by Philip Gross from *The All Nite Café* reprinted by permission of Faber and Faber. **Gregory Harrison:** 'Posting Letters'. Gregory Harrison © first published by Oxford University Press 1968 in *Posting Letters*; reprinted by permission of author. **Michael Harrison:** 'Haircut', 'Sunday Fathers'. By permission of Michael Harrison. **Tessa Hart:** 'Piglet'. From *Wondercrump 3* edited by Jennifer Curry. By permission of Random House. **Seamus Heaney:** 'Follower' from *New Selected Poems 1966-1987* reprinted by permission of Faber and Faber. **Harry Hemsley:** 'The English Language', from *Imagination* by permission of The Lutterworth Press. **Phoebe Hesketh:** 'Clown'. By permission of Phoebe Hesketh: from *The Leave Train: New and Selected Poems* (Enithharmon Press 1994). **Russell Hoban:** 'Egg Thoughts'. By permission of Russell Hoban and Faber and Faber from *Egg Thoughts and Other Frances Songs*. **Kevin Crossley-Holland:** 'Storm at Sea'. By permission of

permission of the author. 'Mary Celeste' by Judith Nicholls from *Midnight Forest*. Reprinted by permission of Faber and Faber. **Riad Nourallah:** 'The Tourists'. By permission of Dr Riad Nourallah. **Gareth Owen:** 'The Alchemist', 'Shed in Space'. By permission of Gareth Owen and Harper Collins Publishers Ltd from *Song of the City*. 'Street Boy', 'Dad' by permission of Rogers, Coleridge & White Ltd. **Sylvia Plath:** 'Mushrooms' from *Collected Poems* by Sylvia Plath. Reprinted by permission of Faber and Faber. **Joan Poulson:** 'First Kiss', 'All That Space'. © Joan Poulson. **John Press:** 'African Christmas'. By permission of John Press & A M Heath & Co Ltd. **James Reeves:** 'The Doze' © James Reeves from *Complete Poems for Children* (Heinemann). Reprinted by permission of James Reeves Estate. **John Rice:** 'Big Fears'. By permission of John Rice. **Albert Rowe:** 'Penguins'. By permission of Albert Rowe. **Carl Sandburg:** 'Circles'. Excerpt from *The People, Yes* by Carl Sandburg, copyright 1936 by Harcourt Brace & Company and renewed 1964 by Carl Sandburg, reprinted by permission of the publisher. **Siegfried Sassoon:** 'The Dug Out', 'The Hero'. Copyright Siegfried Sassoon by permission of George Sassoon. **Vernon Scannell:** 'Fear of the Dark', 'Hide and Seek', 'Growing Pain'. By permission of Vernon Scannell and Robson Books from *Collected Poems 1950-1993*. **Fabiola Smolowik:** 'The Twilight'. From *Wondercrump 3* edited by Jennifer Curry. By permission of Random House. **Rowena Sommerville:** 'Slow Jeanie'. By permission of Rowena Somerville & Hutchinson & Andrew Mann Ltd. **Pauline Stewart:** 'Sauce', 'Skin', 'Our Allotment'. By permission of Pauline Stewart and The Bodley Head from *Singing Down the Breadfruit*. **Geoffrey Summerfield:** 'Washday Battles', 'Reading a bonfire, Top to Bottom'. By permission of the Estate of Geoffrey Summerfield. **Rabindranath Tagore:** 'I Wish I Were' from *The Crescent Moon* by Rabindranath Tagore published by Macmillan. **Barry Wade:** 'Don't', 'The Visitors', 'Coming Late', 'Tall Windows'. By permission of Barry Wade. **John Walsh:** 'The Bully Asleep'. P J Walsh for 'The Bully Asleep' by the late John Herbert Walsh from *Poets in Hand* Puffin. **Tom Wayman:** 'The Feet'. Reprinted by permission of Tom Wayman and Harbour Publishing Co Ltd. **Nancy Willard:** 'Blake Leads a Walk on the Milky Way' from *A Visit to William Blake's Inn*, © 1981 by Nancy Willard, reprinted by permission of Harcourt Brace Company. **Raymond Wilson:** 'Family Holiday'. By permission of Mrs G M Wilson. **John Wright:** 'Baggin''. By permission of John Wright. **W B Yeats:** 'He Wishes for the Cloths of Heaven', 'The Host of the Air'. By permission of A P Watt Ltd on behalf of Michael Yeats. **Benjamin Zephaniah:** 'Talking Turkeys!', 'Civil Lies'. © Benjamin Zephaniah 1994. 'According to My Mood', by permission of Bloodaxe Books.

Every effort has been made to trace copyright holders but in some cases this has not proved possible. The publisher will be happy to rectify any such errors or omissions in future reprints and/or new editions. In particular, we have been unable to contact the following:

Alasdair Aston: 'A Striking Old Man'. **Jean Ayer:** 'Everyday Things'. **James Berry:** 'A Different Kind of Sunday'. **Christine Boothroyd:** 'Down and Out, Paddington Station'. **Jenny Boult:** 'Shopping', 'Shopping Trolleys'. **Dionne Brand:**

'Hurricane'. 'Old Men of Magic'. **Edward Kamau Brathwaite:** 'The Pawpaw'. **Edwin Brock:** 'Song of the Battery Hen'. **David Campbell:** 'Windy Gap'. **Leonard Clark:** 'Heron'. **Afua Cooper:** 'It is Snowing'. **John Cotton:** 'Through that Door'. **Maldwyn Davies:** 'Foodless Children'. **WH Davies:** 'For Sale', 'Leisure, 'A Child's Pet'. **Jan Dean:** 'Uniform'. **Gina Douthwaite:** 'Grave of a Princess'. **Michael Dugan:** 'To a Trainee Accountant'. **William Dunlop:** 'Landscape as Werewolf'. **ARD Fairburn:** 'Song of the Open Road'. **Gilroy Fisher:** 'Zebra'. **Rose Flint:** 'Applemoon'. **Angela Greene:** 'Terrorist's Wife'. **Theresa Heine:** 'An Elephant Remembers'. **AL Hendriks:** 'The Fringe of the Sea'. **Russell Hoban:** 'The Empty House'. **Roy Holland:** 'Hedgehog'. **James Hurley:** 'Greedy Dog'. **Karla Kuskin:** 'Different Dreams'. **John Lacorte:** 'Eternal Love'. **Christopher Leach:** 'Blackbird'. **Norman MacCaig:** 'Sleeping Compartment', 'Uncle Roderick'. **Adam McNaughtan:** 'The Jeely Piece song'. **Barbara Mahone:** 'Sugarfields'. **Gerda Mayer:** '529 1983'. **Trevor Millum:** 'The Song of the Homeworkers'. **Lesley Miranda:** 'Dread-lock Style'. **Charlotte Mitchell:** 'The Passing of the Telegram'. **Pat Moon:** 'Dying Quietly'. **Linda Newton:** 'Lance-corporal Dixon. **Henry Normal:** 'You Never See a Bright Yellow Hearse'. **Wilfred Noyce:** 'Breathless'. **Michael O'Loughlin:** 'Yellow'. **Sharon Olds:** Summer Solstice, New York City'. **Lynn Peters:** 'Why Dorothy Wordsworth is not as famous as her brother'. **Redmond Phillips:** 'Manco the Peruvian Chief'. **Cecil Rajendra:** 'Leave Taking'. **Dudley Randall:** 'Ballad of Birmingham'. **Edith Roseveare:** 'The Statue'. **David Scott:** 'How Does It Feel?'. **Elizabeth Seagar:** 'Death by Sacher Torte'. **Susan Skinner:** 'No Return'. **Darien Smith:** 'Sunstruck'. **William Stafford:** 'Travelling Through the Dark'. **Kaye Starbird:** 'Abigail'. **James Sykes:** 'The dilemmas of AIDS'. **Glyne Walrond:** 'Blackness'. **RP Weston and Bert Lee:** 'With her Head Tucked Underneath'. **Nancy Willard:** 'Magic Story of Falling Asleep'.